Blackstone Outdoor Gas Griddle Cookbook

1000 Days Mouthwatering, Delicious Recipes and Expert Tips for Mastering Your Grill.

Dr Kamilah

TABLE OF CONTENTS

Introduction 7

Recipes 9

    Classic Cheeseburger 9

    Philly Cheesesteak Sandwich 12

    Bacon-Wrapped Jalapeno Poppers 14

    Teriyaki Glazed Salmon 15

    Vegetable Stir-Fr 17

    Grilled Shrimp Tacos 19

    Breakfast Burrito 20

    Grilled Pineapple Slices 22

    Korean BBQ Beef Bulgogi 24

    Grilled Portobello Mushroom Burger 25

    Chicken Fajitas 27

    Buffalo Chicken Wings 29

    Grilled Vegetable Skewers 30

    BBQ Pork Ribs 32

    Grilled Corn on the Cob 34

    Bacon and Cheese Stuffed Burgers 35

    Grilled Flatbread Pizza 37

    Cajun Shrimp and Sausage Skillet 39

    Grilled Teriyaki Chicken 40

    Steak and Cheese Quesadillas 42

Grilled Zucchini and Squash 45

Hawaiian BBQ Chicken Sliders.. 46

Grilled Asparagus 48

Beer-Brined Grilled Pork Chops 49

Grilled BBQ Chicken Pizza.. 52

Korean BBQ Beef Tacos 54

Grilled Watermelon Salad 56

Philly Cheesesteak Stuffed Peppers... 57

Grilled Sweet Potato Fries... 59

BBQ Pulled Pork Sandwiches.. 61

Grilled Caesar Salad 62

Honey Sriracha Glazed Chicken Skewers 64

Grilled Eggplant Parmesan.. 67

Grilled Bratwurst with Sauerkraut 70

Grilled Teriyaki Salmon... 71

Southwest Chicken Quesadillas 73

Grilled Vegetable Panini 75

Grilled Shrimp and Pineapple Skewers... 77

BBQ Bacon-Wrapped Meatloaf 78

Grilled Corn and Black Bean Salad... 80

Garlic Butter Grilled Lobster Tails 81

Grilled Caprese Sandwich 84

Lemon Herb Grilled Chicken.. 86

Grilled Teriyaki Veggie Kabobs 87

BBQ Pulled Chicken Tacos 89

Grilled Romaine Lettuce with Parmesan Dressing 90

Korean BBQ Beef Tacos 92

Grilled Sweet and Spicy Chicken Wings 94

Garlic Butter Grilled Shrimp 96

Grilled Ratatouille 97

Korean BBQ Chicken 99

Grilled Teriyaki Beef Skewers 101

BBQ Bacon-Wrapped Stuffed Jalapenos 103

Grilled Lemon Pepper Chicken 105

Shrimp and Andouille Sausage Jambalaya 106

Grilled Mediterranean Veggie Skewers 109

BBQ Pulled Pork Nachos 110

Grilled Teriyaki Pineapple Chicken 112

Bacon-Wrapped Stuffed Mushrooms 114

Grilled Lemon Garlic Shrimp Scampi Pasta 116

Buffalo Chicken Sliders 118

Grilled Bruschetta Chicken 120

BBQ Pulled Pork Stuffed Sweet Potatoes 121

Grilled Teriyaki Beef Stir-Fry 124

Grilled Cajun Shrimp Po'Boy Sandwich 127

Grilled Honey Mustard Chicken 128

Grilled Stuffed Bell Peppers 130

BBQ Chicken Flatbread Pizza 132

Grilled Pineapple Teriyaki Burgers 133

Bacon-Wrapped BBQ Chicken Skewers 135

Grilled Ratatouille 137

Chipotle Lime Grilled Shrimp 139

Grilled Sausage and Peppers 140

BBQ Pork Sliders 142

Grilled Teriyaki Tofu 144

Portobello Mushroom and Goat Cheese Burger 146

Grilled Mediterranean Chicken Skewers 147

Grilled Caesar Burger 149

Grilled Honey Lime Salmon 151

BBQ Bacon-Wrapped Shrimp 153

Lemon Herb Grilled Pork Chops 156

Grilled Veggie Fajitas 157

BBQ Chicken Flatbread Pizza 159

Grilled Cilantro Lime Shrimp Tacos 162

Grilled Lemon Herb Pork Tenderloin 165

Bacon-Wrapped BBQ Meatballs 166

Grilled Teriyaki Vegetable Fried Rice 168

Grilled Mediterranean Stuffed Peppers 170

BBQ Bacon-Wrapped Stuffed Chicken Breasts 172

Grilled Honey Sriracha Wings 174

Teriyaki Glazed Grilled Pineapple Chicken Skewers 175

Grilled Greek Lamb Burgers 177

BBQ Pulled Chicken Sliders with Coleslaw 179

Grilled Teriyaki Tofu Stir-Fry 181

Conclusion 184

INTRODUCTION

Introducing the "Blackstone Outdoor Gas Griddle Cookbook: 1000 Days Mouthwatering, Delicious Recipes and Expert Tips for Mastering Your Grill." This cookbook is a treasure trove of culinary inspiration for those who love outdoor cooking and want to make the most of their Blackstone outdoor gas grill. With its extensive collection of 1000 recipes, this cookbook offers a wide range of mouthwatering and delicious dishes for every meal of the day.

Whether you're a seasoned griller or just starting, this cookbook is designed to help you elevate your outdoor cooking skills. Alongside the diverse recipe collection, you'll find expert tips and techniques that guide you in mastering your grill. These invaluable insights will teach you how to achieve the perfect sear, control heat zones, and unlock the full potential of your Blackstone gas griddle.

The cookbook is a comprehensive guide that covers various aspects of outdoor griddle cooking. It provides information on griddle setup, essential tools and accessories, and proper maintenance and cleaning techniques. With this knowledge at your fingertips, you'll be equipped to make the most of your grill and create unforgettable meals for your friends and family.

In addition to the wealth of culinary knowledge, this cookbook aims to inspire with its vibrant and enticing food photography. Each recipe is brought to life on the pages, igniting your imagination and motivating you to try new flavours and techniques.

Whether you're craving sizzling steaks, juicy burgers, flavorful stir-fries, or delectable desserts, the "Blackstone Outdoor Gas Griddle Cookbook" has you covered. With its extensive recipe collection, expert tips, and beautiful visuals, this cookbook will become your go-to resource for outdoor griddle cooking. Get ready to embark on a mouthwatering journey and unlock the full potential of your Blackstone gas griddle.

RECIPES

CLASSIC CHEESEBURGER

Prep Time: 15 minutes Cooking Time: 10 minutes Serving: 4 burgers

Ingredients:
- 1 pound ground beef (80% lean)
- One teaspoon salt
- 1/2 teaspoon black pepper
- Four hamburger buns
- Four slices of cheese (cheddar, American, or your choice)
- Optional toppings: lettuce, tomato slices, onion slices, pickles, ketchup, mustard, mayonnaise

Directions:
1. Preheat your grill or stovetop skillet over medium-high heat.
2. In a bowl, season the ground beef with salt and black pepper. Mix gently until the seasoning is evenly distributed.
3. Divide the ground beef into four equal portions and shape them into patties about 1/2 inch thick. Make a slight indentation in the centre of each patty with your thumb to help them cook evenly.

4. Place the patties on the preheated grill or skillet and cook for about 4-5 minutes on each side or until they reach your desired level of doneness.
5. During the last minute of cooking, top each patty with a slice of cheese and let it melt.
6. While the patties are cooking, lightly toast the hamburger buns on the grill or in a toaster.
7. Remove the patties from the heat and let them rest for a few minutes.
8. Assemble the burgers by placing a patty on the bottom half of each bun. Add your preferred toppings, such as lettuce, tomato slices, onion slices, pickles, ketchup, mustard, and mayonnaise.
9. Cover the burgers with the top halves of the buns.
10. Serve the classic cheeseburgers immediately, and enjoy!

Nutrition Facts (per serving):
- Calories: 450
- Total Fat: 24g
- Saturated Fat: 10g
- Cholesterol: 90mg
- Sodium: 900mg
- Carbohydrates: 26g
- Fibre: 1g
- Sugars: 4g
- Protein: 30g

Please note that the nutrition facts may vary depending on the type and amount of toppings you use.

Grilled Chicken Skewers

Prep Time: 20 minutes Cooking Time: 15 minutes Serving: 4 servings

Ingredients:

- 1.5 pounds boneless, skinless chicken breasts cut into 1-inch cubes
- 1/4 cup olive oil
- Two tablespoons of lemon juice
- Two cloves garlic, minced
- One teaspoon of dried oregano
- One teaspoon paprika
- 1/2 teaspoon salt
- 1/4 teaspoon black pepper
- Wooden skewers, soaked in water for 30 minutes

Directions:

1. In a bowl, combine the olive oil, lemon juice, minced garlic, dried oregano, paprika, salt, and black pepper. Mix well to create a marinade.
2. Add the chicken cubes to the marinade and toss until they are well coated. Allow the chicken to marinate for at least 30 minutes in the refrigerator.
3. Preheat your grill to medium-high heat.
4. Thread the marinated chicken cubes onto the soaked wooden skewers.
5. Place the skewers on the preheated grill and cook for about 6-8 minutes per side or until the chicken is cooked through and slightly charred.

6. Once cooked, remove the skewers from the grill and let them rest for a few minutes.
7. Serve the grilled chicken skewers hot with your favourite dipping sauce or a fresh salad or rice.

Nutrition Facts (per serving):
- Calories: 250
- Total Fat: 12g
- Saturated Fat: 2g
- Cholesterol: 80mg
- Sodium: 350mg
- Total Carbohydrate: 2g
- Dietary Fiber: 0g
- Sugars: 0g
- Protein: 32g

Note: Nutrition facts may vary depending on the specific ingredients and brands used.

PHILLY CHEESESTEAK SANDWICH

Prep Time: 15 minutes Cooking Time: 20 minutes Serving: 4

Ingredients:
- 1 pound ribeye steak, thinly sliced
- One green bell pepper, thinly sliced
- One medium onion, thinly sliced
- 8 slices provolone cheese
- Four hoagie rolls
- Two tablespoons of vegetable oil

- Salt and pepper, to taste

Directions:

1. Heat a large skillet over medium-high heat. Add the vegetable oil and let it heat up.
2. Add the thinly sliced ribeye steak to the skillet and cook for 2-3 minutes until browned. Season with salt and pepper to taste. Remove the steak from the skillet and set aside.
3. In the same skillet, add the sliced bell pepper and onion. Cook for 5-7 minutes until the vegetables are soft and slightly caramelized.
4. Return the cooked steak to the skillet with the vegetables. Mix everything and cook for 2-3 minutes to heat the steak.
5. Preheat the oven to 350°F (175°C). Split the hoagie rolls lengthwise and place two slices of provolone cheese on the bottom half of each roll.
6. Place the rolls in the preheated oven for about 5 minutes or until the cheese is melted and the rolls are slightly toasted.
7. Remove the rolls from the oven and spoon the steak and vegetable mixture onto the bottom half of each roll.
8. Close the sandwiches with the top halves of the rolls. Serve immediately.

Nutrition Facts (per serving):

- Calories: 540
- Total Fat: 27g
- Saturated Fat: 12g
- Cholesterol: 95mg
- Sodium: 640mg
- Carbohydrates: 39g

- Fibre: 2g
- Sugars: 6g
- Protein: 34g

Enjoy your delicious Philly Cheesesteak Sandwich!

BACON-WRAPPED JALAPENO POPPERS

Prep Time: 20 minutes Cooking Time: 20 minutes Servings: 6

Ingredients:
- 12 jalapeno peppers
- 6 ounces of cream cheese, softened
- 1 cup shredded cheddar cheese
- 12 slices bacon
- Toothpicks

Directions:
1. Preheat your oven to 400°F (200°C). Line a baking sheet with aluminium foil and set aside.
2. Slice each jalapeno pepper in half lengthwise. Remove the seeds and membranes using a spoon. Wear gloves or wash your hands thoroughly afterwards to avoid irritation.
3. Combine the softened cream cheese and shredded cheddar cheese in a mixing bowl. Mix until well combined.
4. Fill each jalapeno half with the cream cheese mixture using a spoon or piping bag.
5. Wrap each stuffed jalapeno half with a slice of bacon, securing it with a toothpick.
6. Arrange the bacon-wrapped jalapeno poppers on the prepared baking sheet.

7. Bake in the preheated oven for about 20 minutes or until the bacon is crispy and the peppers are tender.
8. Remove from the oven and let them cool for a few minutes before serving.
9. Serve the bacon-wrapped jalapeno poppers as an appetizer or snack. Remove the toothpicks before eating.

Nutrition Facts (per serving):
- Calories: 240
- Fat: 20g
- Saturated Fat: 10g
- Cholesterol: 60mg
- Sodium: 440mg
- Carbohydrates: 3g
- Fibre: 1g
- Sugar: 2g
- Protein: 11g

Note: The nutrition facts are approximate and may vary based on the specific ingredients used.

TERIYAKI GLAZED SALMON

Prep Time: 15 minutes Cooking Time: 20 minutes Serving: 4 servings

Ingredients:
- Four salmon fillets
- 1/4 cup soy sauce
- 1/4 cup mirin (Japanese sweet rice wine)
- Two tablespoons honey

- One tablespoon of rice vinegar
- One tablespoon of sesame oil
- Two cloves garlic, minced
- One teaspoon of grated ginger
- One tablespoon cornstarch
- Two tablespoons water
- Sesame seeds, for garnish
- Green onions, sliced, for garnish
- Steamed white rice or cooked noodles for serving

Directions:

1. In a small bowl, whisk together soy sauce, mirin, honey, rice vinegar, sesame oil, garlic, and ginger to make the teriyaki sauce.
2. Place the salmon fillets in a shallow dish and pour half of the teriyaki sauce over them. Marinate for at least 10 minutes or up to 30 minutes for more flavour.
3. Preheat the oven to 400°F (200°C).
4. Heat a large oven-safe skillet over medium-high heat. Add a drizzle of oil to the pan and swirl to coat.
5. Remove the salmon from the marinade, reserving the marinade for later. Place the salmon fillets in the hot skillet, skin-side down. Sear for 2-3 minutes until the skin is crispy and browned.
6. Flip the salmon fillets and brush the tops with some reserved teriyaki sauce. Transfer the skillet to the preheated oven and bake for 10-12 minutes, or until the salmon is cooked through and flakes easily with a fork.

7. While the salmon is cooking, pour the remaining teriyaki sauce into a small saucepan. In a separate small bowl, whisk together the cornstarch and water until smooth. Add the cornstarch mixture to the saucepan and bring the sauce to a simmer over medium heat. Cook for 2-3 minutes or until the sauce thickens. Remove from heat.
8. Once the salmon is done, remove it from the oven and brush it with more of the teriyaki glaze. Sprinkle with sesame seeds and sliced green onions for garnish.
9. Serve the teriyaki glazed salmon over steamed white rice or cooked noodles drizzled with the remaining teriyaki sauce. Enjoy!

Nutrition Facts (per serving): Calories: 350 Total Fat: 16g Saturated Fat: 3g Cholesterol: 80mg Sodium: 800mg Carbohydrates: 19g Fiber: 0.5g Sugar: 14g Protein: 32g

VEGETABLE STIR-FR

Prep Time: 15 minutes Cooking Time: 10 minutes Serving: 4

Ingredients:
- Two tablespoons of vegetable oil
- One onion, thinly sliced
- Two cloves garlic, minced
- One red bell pepper, sliced
- One yellow bell pepper, sliced
- One carrot, julienned
- One zucchini, sliced
- 1 cup broccoli florets
- 1 cup snow peas

- 1 cup mushrooms, sliced
- 1/4 cup soy sauce
- Two tablespoons of oyster sauce
- One tablespoon of sesame oil
- One tablespoon cornstarch dissolved in 2 tablespoons of water
- Salt and pepper to taste

Directions:
1. Heat the vegetable oil in a large skillet or wok over medium-high heat.
2. Add the onion and garlic to the skillet and sauté for 2-3 minutes until the onion becomes translucent.
3. Add the bell peppers, carrot, zucchini, broccoli, snow peas, and mushrooms to the skillet. Stir-fry for about 5 minutes or until the vegetables are crisp-tender.
4. Whisk together the soy sauce, oyster sauce, sesame oil, and cornstarch mixture in a small bowl.
5. Pour the sauce over the vegetables in the skillet and stir well to coat. Cook for an additional 2 minutes until the sauce thickens.
6. Season with salt and pepper to taste.
7. Remove from heat and serve the vegetable stir-fry hot with steamed rice or noodles.

Nutrition Facts (per serving):
- Calories: 180
- Total Fat: 9g
- Saturated Fat: 1g
- Cholesterol: 0mg

- Sodium: 800mg
- Total Carbohydrate: 21g
- Dietary Fiber: 6g
- Sugars: 8g
- Protein: 6g

Note: Nutrition facts may vary depending on the specific brands and quantities of ingredients used.

GRILLED SHRIMP TACOS

Prep Time: 15 minutes Cooking Time: 10 minutes Serving: 4

Ingredients:

- 1 pound large shrimp, peeled and deveined
- Two tablespoons of olive oil
- One tablespoon of lime juice
- One teaspoon of chilli powder
- One teaspoon cumin
- 1/2 teaspoon garlic powder
- Salt and pepper, to taste
- Eight small flour tortillas
- 1 cup shredded lettuce
- 1/2 cup diced tomatoes
- 1/4 cup diced red onion
- 1/4 cup chopped fresh cilantro
- Lime wedges for serving

Directions:

1. In a bowl, combine the olive oil, lime juice, chilli powder, cumin, garlic powder, salt, and pepper. Add the shrimp to the bowl and toss until well-coated. Let the shrimp marinate for 10 minutes.
2. Preheat the grill to medium-high heat.
3. Thread the marinated shrimp onto skewers, if desired, or place them directly on the grill grates. Grill the shrimp for about 2-3 minutes per side until they are pink and cooked through.
4. While the shrimp is grilling, warm the tortillas on the grill or in a dry skillet over medium heat until they are soft and pliable.
5. Remove the shrimp from the grill and let them cool for a minute. Remove the shrimp from the skewers if using.
6. To assemble the tacos, place a few shrimp on each tortilla. Top with shredded lettuce, diced tomatoes, red onion, and chopped cilantro. Squeeze fresh lime juice over the top.
7. Serve the grilled shrimp tacos with lime wedges on the side.

Nutrition Facts (per serving): Calories: 290 Total Fat: 10g Saturated Fat: 1.5g Cholesterol: 170mg Sodium: 520mg Carbohydrates: 28g Fiber: 3g Sugar: 3g Protein: 22g

Note: Nutrition facts may vary depending on the specific ingredients and brands used.

BREAKFAST BURRITO

Prep Time: 10 minutes Cooking Time: 15 minutes Serving: 2
Ingredients:
- Four large eggs

- 1/4 cup milk
- Salt and pepper to taste
- Two large flour tortillas
- 1/2 cup shredded cheddar cheese
- Four slices of cooked bacon crumbled
- 1/4 cup diced tomatoes
- Two tablespoons chopped fresh cilantro
- Salsa, for serving

Directions:

1. In a bowl, whisk together the eggs, milk, salt, and pepper until well combined.
2. Heat a non-stick skillet over medium heat and coat it with cooking spray or a small amount of oil.
3. Pour the egg mixture into the skillet and cook, stirring occasionally, until the eggs are scrambled and cooked. Remove from heat.
4. Warm the flour tortillas in a microwave or on a stovetop until they are pliable.
5. Divide the scrambled eggs between the two tortillas, placing them in the centre.
6. Sprinkle shredded cheese, crumbled bacon, diced tomatoes, and chopped cilantro over the eggs.
7. Fold the sides of the tortillas over the filling, then roll them up tightly to form burritos.
8. Heat a large skillet over medium heat and place the burritos, seam-side down, in the skillet. Cook for 2-3 minutes on each side or until the tortillas are lightly browned and crispy.

9. Remove the burritos from the skillet and let them cool for a minute. Cut each burrito in half diagonally.
10. Serve the breakfast burritos with salsa on the side, and enjoy!

Nutrition Facts (per serving):

- Calories: 430
- Total Fat: 27g
- Saturated Fat: 10g
- Cholesterol: 350mg
- Sodium: 860mg
- Total Carbohydrate: 22g
- Dietary Fiber: 2g
- Sugars: 2g
- Protein: 25g

Note: The nutrition facts are approximate and may vary depending on the specific brands of ingredients used.

GRILLED PINEAPPLE SLICES

Prep Time: 10 minutes Cooking Time: 8 minutes Serving: 4

Ingredients:

- One ripe pineapple
- Two tablespoons honey
- One tablespoon of lime juice
- One teaspoon of ground cinnamon
- Optional toppings: vanilla ice cream, chopped mint leaves

Directions:

1. Preheat your grill to medium-high heat.
2. Slice off the top and bottom of the pineapple, then carefully cut off the skin, making sure to remove any "eyes" (hard spots) on the surface. Cut the pineapple into 1/2-inch thick slices.
3. In a small bowl, whisk together the honey, lime juice, and ground cinnamon until well combined.
4. Brush both sides of each pineapple slice with the honey-lime mixture, ensuring they are evenly coated.
5. Place the pineapple slices directly on the preheated grill. Grill for about 4 minutes on each side or until grill marks appear and the pineapple caramelizes slightly.
6. Remove the grilled pineapple slices from the grill and transfer them to a serving platter.
7. If desired, serve the grilled pineapple slices with a scoop of vanilla ice cream on top and sprinkle with chopped mint leaves for added freshness.
8. Enjoy your delicious grilled pineapple slices!

Nutrition Facts (per serving):

- Calories: 120
- Total Fat: 0.5g
- Cholesterol: 0mg
- Sodium: 0mg
- Total Carbohydrate: 32g
- Dietary Fiber: 2g
- Sugars: 25g
- Protein: 1g

Note: The nutrition facts may vary depending on the size of the pineapple and the amount of honey used.

KOREAN BBQ BEEF BULGOGI

Prep Time: 15 minutes Cooking Time: 10 minutes Serving: 4

Ingredients:
- 1.5 pounds (700 grams) of beef sirloin, thinly sliced
- 1/2 cup soy sauce
- 1/4 cup brown sugar
- Two tablespoons of sesame oil
- Three cloves garlic, minced
- One tablespoon of grated ginger
- Two tablespoons rice wine (or mirin)
- One tablespoon honey
- Two green onions, thinly sliced
- One teaspoon of toasted sesame seeds
- 1/4 teaspoon black pepper
- Two tablespoons of vegetable oil

Directions:
1. In a bowl, whisk together soy sauce, brown sugar, sesame oil, minced garlic, grated ginger, rice wine (or mirin), honey, green onions, sesame seeds, and black pepper to make the marinade.
2. Place the thinly sliced beef in a large ziplock bag and pour the marinade over it. Close the bag tightly and gently massage the beef to ensure it's evenly coated with the marinade. Let

it marinate in the refrigerator for at least 1 hour or overnight for maximum flavour.

3. Heat the vegetable oil in a large skillet or grill pan over medium-high heat.
4. Remove the beef from the marinade, allowing any excess marinade to drip off, and add it to the hot skillet. Cook for about 3-4 minutes, stirring occasionally, until the beef is cooked and slightly caramelized.
5. Transfer the cooked beef bulgogi to a serving plate and garnish with additional sliced green onions and sesame seeds, if desired.
6. Serve the Korean BBQ Beef Bulgogi with steamed rice and your choice of side dishes, such as kimchi and pickled vegetables.

Nutrition Facts (per serving):

- Calories: 360
- Total Fat: 16g
- Saturated Fat: 4g
- Cholesterol: 85mg
- Sodium: 1160mg
- Carbohydrate: 20g
- Fibre: 1g
- Sugar: 15g
- Protein: 35g

Enjoy your delicious Korean BBQ Beef Bulgogi!

GRILLED PORTOBELLO MUSHROOM BURGER

Prep Time: 15 minutes Cooking Time: 15 minutes Serving: 4 burgers

Ingredients:

- Four large Portobello mushroom caps
- Four burger buns
- Four slices of Swiss cheese (optional)
- One red onion, sliced
- One large tomato, sliced
- Handful of lettuce leaves
- Pickles (optional)
- Four tablespoons of olive oil
- Two tablespoons of balsamic vinegar
- Two cloves of garlic, minced
- Salt and pepper to taste

Directions:

1. Preheat your grill or grill pan to medium-high heat.
2. Whisk together olive oil, balsamic vinegar, minced garlic, salt, and pepper in a small bowl.
3. Brush the mushroom caps with the prepared marinade on both sides.
4. Place the mushrooms on the grill and cook for about 4-5 minutes per side until they are tender and have grill marks.
5. While the mushrooms are grilling, lightly toast the burger buns on the grill.
6. If desired, place a slice of Swiss cheese on each mushroom cap during the last minute of grilling to melt.

7. Remove the mushrooms from the grill and let them rest for a few minutes.
8. Assemble the burgers by placing a Portobello mushroom cap on the bottom half of each bun.
9. Top with sliced red onion, tomato, lettuce leaves, and pickles, if desired.
10. Cover with the top half of the bun.
11. Serve the Grilled Portobello Mushroom Burgers immediately, and enjoy!

Nutrition Facts (per serving):
- Calories: 250
- Total Fat: 14g
- Saturated Fat: 2g
- Cholesterol: 0mg
- Sodium: 200mg
- Total Carbohydrate: 28g
- Dietary Fiber: 5g
- Sugars: 6g
- Protein: 7g

Note: Nutrition facts may vary depending on the specific ingredients and brands used.

CHICKEN FAJITAS

Prep Time: 15 minutes Cooking Time: 20 minutes Serving: 4

Ingredients:
- 1 lb (450g) boneless, skinless chicken breasts cut into thin strips

- One red bell pepper, sliced
- One green bell pepper, sliced
- One yellow bell pepper, sliced
- One onion, sliced
- Three cloves of garlic, minced
- Two tablespoons of olive oil
- Two tablespoons of fajita seasoning
- Salt and pepper, to taste
- Eight small flour tortillas
- Optional toppings: sour cream, guacamole, shredded cheese, salsa

Directions:

1. In a large bowl, combine the chicken strips, sliced bell peppers, onion, minced garlic, olive oil, fajita seasoning, salt, and pepper. Toss everything together until the chicken and vegetables are well coated with the seasoning.
2. Heat a large skillet or grill pan over medium-high heat. Add the chicken and vegetables mixture to the pan and cook for about 10-12 minutes, or until the chicken is cooked and the vegetables are tender, stirring occasionally.
3. While the chicken and vegetables are cooking, warm the flour tortillas according to the package instructions or heat them on a dry skillet for a few seconds on each side.
4. Once the chicken and vegetables are cooked, remove the skillet from the heat.
5. Serve the chicken fajita mixture on warm tortillas. Add your desired toppings, such as sour cream, guacamole, shredded cheese, and salsa.

6. Roll up the tortillas, tucking in the sides, to form fajitas. Serve immediately.

Nutrition Facts (per serving):
- Calories: 380
- Fat: 12g
- Saturated Fat: 2.5g
- Cholesterol: 80mg
- Sodium: 650mg
- Carbohydrates: 34g
- Fibre: 5g
- Sugar: 5g
- Protein: 32g

Note: Nutrition facts may vary depending on the specific brands of ingredients used and any additional toppings added.

BUFFALO CHICKEN WINGS

Prep Time: 10 minutes Cooking Time: 45 minutes Serving: 4

Ingredients:
- 2 pounds (about 900 grams) of chicken wings
- 1/2 cup all-purpose flour
- One teaspoon of garlic powder
- One teaspoon paprika
- 1/2 teaspoon salt
- 1/2 teaspoon black pepper
- 1/4 cup unsalted butter, melted
- 1/2 cup hot sauce (such as Frank's RedHot)

- Blue cheese or ranch dressing for serving
- Celery sticks for serving

Directions:
1. Preheat the oven to 400°F (200°C). Line a baking sheet with aluminium foil and set aside.
2. In a large bowl, combine the flour, garlic powder, paprika, salt, and black pepper. Toss the chicken wings in the flour mixture, ensuring they are well coated.
3. Place the coated wings on the prepared baking sheet and bake in the preheated oven for 40-45 minutes or until they are crispy and golden brown.
4. While the wings are baking, mix the melted butter and hot sauce in a separate bowl.
5. Once the wings are cooked, transfer them to a large bowl and pour the hot sauce mixture over them. Toss the wings until they are evenly coated with the sauce.
6. Serve the Buffalo chicken wings with blue cheese or ranch dressing on the side for dipping. Also, provide celery sticks for a refreshing accompaniment.
7. Enjoy your delicious Buffalo Chicken Wings!

Nutrition Facts: Note: Nutritional information may vary depending on the specific ingredients and brands used.

Please consult a nutritionist or use online nutritional calculators for the most accurate information.

I hope you enjoy making and eating these Buffalo Chicken Wings!

GRILLED VEGETABLE SKEWERS

Prep Time: 20 minutes Cooking Time: 15 minutes Serving: 4 servings

Ingredients:
- Two bell peppers (any colour), seeded and cut into chunks
- One large zucchini, sliced
- One large red onion, cut into chunks
- Eight cherry tomatoes
- Eight button mushrooms
- Two tablespoons olive oil
- Two tablespoons balsamic vinegar
- Two cloves garlic, minced
- One teaspoon dried oregano
- Salt and pepper, to taste
- Wooden or metal skewers

Directions:
1. Preheat your grill to medium-high heat.
2. In a small bowl, whisk together the olive oil, balsamic vinegar, minced garlic, dried oregano, salt, and pepper.
3. Thread the vegetables onto skewers, alternating between peppers, zucchini, onion, tomatoes, and mushrooms. Leave a little space between each piece to ensure even cooking.
4. Brush the vegetable skewers with the prepared marinade, and coat them well on all sides.
5. Place the skewers on the preheated grill and cook for about 10-15 minutes, turning occasionally, until the vegetables are tender and slightly charred.

6. Once cooked, remove the skewers from the grill and let them cool for a few minutes before serving.
7. Serve the grilled vegetable skewers as a side dish or as a main course with rice, quinoa, or a salad.

Nutrition Facts (per serving): Calories: 120 Total Fat: 7g

- Saturated Fat: 1g
- Trans Fat: 0g Cholesterol: 0mg Sodium: 30mg Total Carbohydrate: 13g
- Dietary Fiber: 4g
- Sugars: 7g Protein: 3g

Note: The nutrition facts are approximate and may vary depending on the ingredients used.

BBQ PORK RIBS

Prep Time: 15 minutes Cooking Time: 2 hours Servings: 4

Ingredients:

- Two racks of pork ribs (about 4 pounds)
- One tablespoon brown sugar
- One tablespoon paprika
- One tablespoon garlic powder
- One tablespoon onion powder
- One teaspoon salt
- One teaspoon black pepper
- One teaspoon chili powder
- 1 cup barbecue sauce

Directions:

1. Preheat your grill to medium heat.
2. In a small bowl, combine the brown sugar, paprika, garlic powder, onion powder, salt, black pepper, and chilli powder. Mix well to create a dry rub.
3. Place the pork ribs on a large baking sheet or cutting board. Rub the dry rub mixture all over the ribs, coating them evenly.
4. Place the ribs on the preheated grill and cook for about 1.5 to 2 hours, or until the meat is tender and starts to pull away from the bones. Make sure to flip the ribs every 30 minutes to ensure even cooking.
5. During the last 10 minutes of cooking, brush the barbecue sauce onto the ribs, coating them generously. This will create a flavorful glaze.
6. Once the ribs are cooked, and the sauce has caramelized slightly, remove them from the grill and let them rest for a few minutes.
7. Cut the ribs into individual portions and serve hot. You can serve them with additional barbecue sauce on the side if desired.

Nutrition Facts (per serving):
- Calories: 550
- Fat: 32g
- Saturated Fat: 10g
- Cholesterol: 140mg
- Sodium: 850mg
- Carbohydrates: 16g
- Fibre: 1g

- Sugar: 13g
- Protein: 47g

Enjoy your delicious BBQ Pork Ribs!

GRILLED CORN ON THE COB

Prep Time: 10 minutes Cooking Time: 15 minutes Serving: 4 servings

Ingredients:
- Four ears of corn
- Two tablespoons olive oil
- Salt and pepper to taste
- Two tablespoons butter, softened
- Optional toppings: grated Parmesan cheese, chopped fresh herbs (such as parsley or cilantro), lime wedges

Directions:
1. Preheat your grill to medium-high heat.
2. Peel back the husks of the corn, but leave them attached at the base. Remove the silk threads from the corn and discard.
3. Brush each ear of corn with olive oil, making sure to coat all sides. Sprinkle with salt and pepper according to your taste.
4. Pull the husks back over the corn and tie them with kitchen twine or a strip of corn husk to keep them in place.
5. Place the corn on the preheated grill and cook for about 15 minutes, turning occasionally, until the kernels are tender and slightly charred.
6. Remove the corn from the grill and carefully peel back the husks. Be cautious, as the corn will be hot.

7. Spread a small amount of softened butter over each ear of corn. You can also sprinkle grated Parmesan cheese, chopped fresh herbs, or squeeze lime juice over the corn for added flavour.

8. Serve the grilled corn on the cob immediately while it's still hot. Enjoy!

Nutrition Facts (per serving):
- Calories: 180
- Total Fat: 10g
- Saturated Fat: 4g
- Cholesterol: 15mg
- Sodium: 60mg
- Carbohydrates: 23g
- Fibre: 3g
- Sugar: 5g
- Protein: 4g

Note: Nutrition facts may vary depending on the size of the corn and the amount of toppings used.

BACON AND CHEESE STUFFED BURGERS

Prep Time: 15 minutes Cooking Time: 15 minutes Serving: 4 burgers

Ingredients:
- 1 pound ground beef
- Eight slices bacon
- Four slices cheddar cheese
- 1/2 teaspoon salt

- 1/2 teaspoon black pepper
- 1/2 teaspoon garlic powder
- Four hamburger buns
- Lettuce, tomato, onions (optional, for garnish)
- Ketchup, mustard (optional, for serving)

Directions:

1. Preheat your grill or stovetop grill pan to medium-high heat.
2. In a mixing bowl, combine the ground beef, salt, black pepper, and garlic powder. Mix well until the spices are evenly incorporated into the meat.
3. Divide the meat mixture into eight equal portions. Take one portion of meat and shape it into a patty using your hands. Repeat with the remaining portions to form 4 patties in total.
4. Take a slice of bacon and wrap it around the edges of one patty, ensuring that the edges of the bacon overlap slightly. Repeat with the other patties and bacon slices.
5. Place the bacon-wrapped patties on the preheated grill or grill pan. Cook for about 5-6 minutes per side or until the burgers are cooked to your desired level of doneness.
6. During the last minute of cooking, place a slice of cheddar cheese on top of each patty. Cover the grill or pan to allow the cheese to melt slightly.
7. While the burgers are cooking, lightly toast the hamburger buns on the grill or in a toaster.
8. Remove the burgers from the heat and let them rest for a few minutes. This allows the juices to redistribute and makes the burgers juicier.

9. Assemble the burgers by placing each patty on a toasted bun. Add lettuce, tomato, onions, ketchup, mustard, or any other desired toppings.
10. Serve the bacon and cheese stuffed burgers hot, and enjoy!

Nutrition Facts (per serving): Calories: 490 Total Fat: 28g

- Saturated Fat: 11g
- Trans Fat: 1g Cholesterol: 110mg Sodium: 900mg Total Carbohydrate: 22g
- Dietary Fiber: 1g
- Sugars: 3g Protein: 36g

Note: Nutrition facts may vary depending on the specific ingredients and brands used.

GRILLED FLATBREAD PIZZA

Prep Time: 15 minutes Cooking Time: 10 minutes Serving: 4 servings

Ingredients:

- Four pieces of flatbread (approximately 8 inches in diameter)
- 1 cup pizza sauce
- 2 cups shredded mozzarella cheese
- 1 cup sliced bell peppers
- 1 cup sliced mushrooms
- 1/2 cup sliced black olives
- 1/2 cup sliced pepperoni or cooked chicken (optional)
- Fresh basil leaves for garnish (optional)

Directions:
1. Preheat your grill to medium-high heat.
2. Place the flatbread on a clean working surface.
3. Spread approximately 1/4 cup of pizza sauce evenly on each flatbread.
4. Sprinkle about 1/2 cup of shredded mozzarella cheese on top of the sauce on each flatbread.
5. Add your desired toppings, such as sliced bell peppers, mushrooms, black olives, and pepperoni or cooked chicken.
6. Carefully transfer the prepared flatbread onto the preheated grill.
7. Close the grill and cook for about 8-10 minutes or until the cheese is melted and bubbly and the flatbread is crispy.
8. Remove the grilled flatbread pizzas from the grill and let them cool for a minute or two.
9. Cut each flatbread pizza into quarters or smaller slices if preferred.
10. Garnish with fresh basil leaves if desired.
11. Serve immediately and enjoy!

Nutrition Facts (per serving):
- Calories: 350
- Fat: 16g
- Saturated Fat: 8g
- Cholesterol: 40mg
- Sodium: 780mg
- Carbohydrates: 35g
- Fibre: 4g

- Sugar: 5g
- Protein: 18g

Note: Nutrition facts may vary depending on the specific brands and quantities of ingredients used.

CAJUN SHRIMP AND SAUSAGE SKILLET

Prep Time: 15 minutes Cooking Time: 20 minutes Serving: 4 servings

Ingredients:
- 1 pound shrimp, peeled and deveined
- 1 pound smoked sausage, sliced
- One bell pepper, thinly sliced
- One onion, thinly sliced
- Three cloves garlic, minced
- Two tablespoons Cajun seasoning
- One teaspoon paprika
- 1/2 teaspoon dried thyme
- 1/2 teaspoon dried oregano
- 1/4 teaspoon cayenne pepper (adjust to taste)
- Two tablespoons olive oil
- Salt and pepper to taste
- Fresh parsley, chopped (for garnish)

Directions:
1. In a small bowl, combine the Cajun seasoning, paprika, dried thyme, oregano, cayenne pepper, salt, and pepper. Set aside.
2. Heat olive oil in a large skillet over medium-high heat.

3. Add the sliced sausage to the skillet and cook until browned about 5 minutes.
4. Remove the sausage from the skillet and set aside.
5. Add bell pepper, onion, and minced garlic in the same skillet. Sauté until the vegetables are tender, about 5 minutes.
6. Add the shrimp to the skillet and sprinkle the Cajun seasoning mixture. Cook for 2-3 minutes, until the shrimp turn pink and are cooked through.
7. Return the cooked sausage to the skillet and toss everything together to combine. Cook for an additional 2 minutes to heat through.
8. Remove from heat and garnish with fresh parsley.
9. Serve the Cajun Shrimp and Sausage Skillet hot with rice or crusty bread.

Nutrition Facts (per serving):
- Calories: 350
- Fat: 22g
- Cholesterol: 180mg
- Sodium: 1200mg
- Carbohydrates: 12g
- Fibre: 2g
- Protein: 28g

Note: The nutrition facts provided are estimates and may vary based on the specific ingredients used.

GRILLED TERIYAKI CHICKEN

Prep Time: 15 minutes Cooking Time: 20 minutes Serving: 4

Ingredients:
- Four boneless, skinless chicken breasts
- 1/2 cup soy sauce
- 1/4 cup honey
- 1/4 cup rice vinegar
- Two tablespoons sesame oil
- Two cloves garlic, minced
- One teaspoon grated fresh ginger
- One tablespoon cornstarch
- Two tablespoons water
- Sesame seeds, for garnish (optional)
- Sliced green onions for garnish (optional)

Directions:
1. In a bowl, whisk together soy sauce, honey, rice vinegar, sesame oil, minced garlic, and grated ginger to make the teriyaki marinade.
2. Place the chicken breasts in a shallow dish or a resealable plastic bag. Pour the teriyaki marinade over the chicken, ensuring each breast is coated evenly. Marinate in the refrigerator for at least 1 hour or overnight for maximum flavour.
3. Preheat your grill to medium-high heat.
4. Remove the chicken from the marinade and shake off any excess liquid. Reserve the marinade for later use.
5. Grill the chicken breasts for about 6-8 minutes per side or until they reach an internal temperature of 165°F (75°C). Baste the chicken occasionally with the reserved marinade during cooking.

6. While the chicken grills pour the remaining marinade into a small saucepan; in a separate bowl, mix cornstarch and water until smooth. Add the cornstarch mixture to the saucepan and bring the marinade to a boil over medium heat, stirring constantly. Cook for 1-2 minutes or until the sauce thickens.
7. Once the chicken is cooked, remove it from the grill and let it rest for a few minutes.
8. Slice the grilled chicken and drizzle the teriyaki sauce on top. Garnish with sesame seeds and sliced green onions, if desired.
9. Serve the Grilled Teriyaki Chicken with steamed rice and your choice of vegetables.

Nutrition Facts (per serving): Calories: 250 Total Fat: 7g Saturated Fat: 1.5g Cholesterol: 90mg Sodium: 1100mg Total Carbohydrate: 15g Dietary Fiber: 0.5g Sugar: 12g Protein: 32g

Note: The nutrition facts are approximate and may vary depending on the ingredients used.

STEAK AND CHEESE QUESADILLAS

Prep Time: 15 minutes Cooking Time: 20 minutes Serving: 4 quesadillas

Ingredients:
- 1 lb (450 g) steak (sirloin, ribeye, or flank steak), thinly sliced
- One tablespoon vegetable oil
- One bell pepper, thinly sliced
- One small onion, thinly sliced
- Two cloves garlic, minced

- One teaspoon chili powder
- 1/2 teaspoon cumin
- Salt and pepper, to taste
- Four large flour tortillas
- 2 cups shredded cheese (cheddar, Monterey Jack, or a combination)
- Salsa, sour cream, and guacamole for serving (optional)

Directions:

1. In a large skillet, heat the vegetable oil over medium-high heat. Add the steak slices and cook for about 3-4 minutes until browned. Remove the steak from the skillet and set aside.
2. Add bell pepper, onion, and garlic in the same skillet. Sauté for 3-4 minutes until the vegetables are slightly tender.
3. Return the cooked steak to the skillet with the vegetables. Sprinkle chilli powder, cumin, salt, and pepper over the mixture. Stir well to combine and cook for another 2 minutes. Remove from heat.
4. Preheat a separate skillet or griddle over medium heat.
5. Place one flour tortilla on the skillet and sprinkle a quarter of the shredded cheese evenly over the tortilla.
6. Spoon a quarter of the steak and vegetable mixture onto half the tortilla. Fold the other half over the filling to create a half-moon shape.
7. Cook the quesadilla for 2-3 minutes on each side until the tortilla is golden brown and the cheese is melted. Repeat the process with the remaining tortillas and filling.
8. Once cooked, remove the quesadillas from the skillet and let them cool for a minute. Cut each quesadilla into wedges.

9. Serve the steak and cheese quesadillas with salsa, sour cream, and guacamole, if desired.

Nutrition Facts (per serving): Calories: 450 Total Fat: 24g Saturated Fat: 10g Cholesterol: 85mg Sodium: 600mg Carbohydrates: 28g Fiber: 3g Sugar: 3g Protein: 30g

Enjoy your delicious Steak and Cheese Quesadillas!

GRILLED ZUCCHINI AND SQUASH

Prep Time: 15 minutes Cooking Time: 10 minutes Serving: 4 servings

Ingredients:

- Two medium zucchini
- Two medium yellow squash
- Two tablespoons olive oil
- Two cloves garlic, minced
- One teaspoon dried Italian seasoning
- Salt and pepper to taste
- Fresh parsley for garnish (optional)

Directions:

1. Preheat your grill to medium-high heat.
2. Wash the zucchini and squash, then trim off the ends. Cut them into 1/4-inch thick slices lengthwise.
3. In a small bowl, combine the olive oil, minced garlic, dried Italian seasoning, salt, and pepper. Mix well.
4. Brush both sides of the zucchini and squash slices with the olive oil.
5. Place the zucchini and squash slices on the preheated grill. Cook for about 4-5 minutes per side or until they are tender and have grill marks.
6. Once cooked, remove the zucchini and squash from the grill and transfer them to a serving platter.
7. Optional: Garnish with fresh parsley for added flavour and presentation.

8. Serve the grilled zucchini and squash as a side dish or as a topping for salads, sandwiches, or wraps.

Nutrition Facts: Serving Size: 1/4 of the recipe Calories: 90 Total Fat: 7g

- Saturated Fat: 1g
- Trans Fat: 0g Cholesterol: 0mg Sodium: 5mg Total Carbohydrate: 6g
- Dietary Fiber: 2g
- Sugars: 3g Protein: 2g

Note: Nutrition information may vary depending on the specific ingredients and quantities used.

HAWAIIAN BBQ CHICKEN SLIDERS

Prep Time: 15 minutes Cooking Time: 20 minutes Serving: 4-6 servings

Ingredients:

- 1.5 lbs (680 g) boneless, skinless chicken breasts
- 1 cup pineapple juice
- 1/2 cup barbecue sauce
- 1/4 cup soy sauce
- Two tablespoons brown sugar
- One tablespoon Worcestershire sauce
- One teaspoon garlic powder
- 1/2 teaspoon ground ginger
- Salt and pepper to taste
- Slider buns
- Pineapple slices (optional)

- Lettuce leaves (optional)
- Red onion slices (optional)

Directions:

1. In a bowl, whisk together the pineapple juice, barbecue sauce, soy sauce, brown sugar, Worcestershire sauce, garlic powder, ground ginger, salt, and pepper.
2. Place the chicken breasts in a resealable plastic bag and pour in the marinade. Seal the bag and refrigerate for at least 2 hours or overnight for best results.
3. Preheat your grill or stovetop grill pan over medium heat.
4. Remove the chicken from the marinade and discard the marinade.
5. Grill the chicken for about 6-8 minutes per side or until cooked through and no longer pink in the centre. The internal temperature should reach 165°F (74°C).
6. Once cooked, remove the chicken from the grill and let it rest for a few minutes. Then, slice the chicken into thin strips or shred it using two forks.
7. Toast the slider buns on the grill for a minute or until slightly crispy.
8. Assemble the sliders by placing a few slices of chicken on the bottom half of each bun. Add a pineapple slice, lettuce leaf, and red onion slice if desired. Top with the other half of the bun.
9. Serve the Hawaiian BBQ chicken sliders immediately, and enjoy!

Nutrition Facts (per serving):

- Calories: 320
- Fat: 4g

- Saturated Fat: 1g
- Cholesterol: 80mg
- Sodium: 900mg
- Carbohydrates: 38g
- Fibre: 2g
- Sugar: 22g
- Protein: 34g

Note: Nutrition facts may vary depending on the specific brands of ingredients used and the serving size.

GRILLED ASPARAGUS

Prep Time: 10 minutes Cooking Time: 10 minutes Serving: 4 servings

Ingredients:
- 1 pound (450g) asparagus spears, woody ends trimmed
- Two tablespoons olive oil
- Two cloves garlic, minced
- Salt and pepper, to taste
- Lemon wedges for serving (optional)

Directions:
1. Preheat your grill to medium-high heat.
2. In a large bowl, combine the asparagus spears, olive oil, minced garlic, salt, and pepper. Toss well to evenly coat the asparagus.
3. Place the asparagus spears directly on the preheated grill grates. Cook for about 4-5 minutes, or until they are tender

and slightly charred, turning occasionally to ensure even cooking.
4. Once grilled to your desired tenderness, remove the asparagus from the grill and transfer them to a serving platter.
5. Serve the grilled asparagus hot, optionally accompanied by lemon wedges for squeezing over the asparagus.

Nutrition Facts (per serving):

- Calories: 80
- Total Fat: 7g
- Saturated Fat: 1g
- Cholesterol: 0mg
- Sodium: 0mg
- Total Carbohydrate: 4g
- Dietary Fiber: 2g
- Sugars: 2g
- Protein: 2g

Note: The nutrition facts are approximate and may vary based on the specific ingredients used.

BEER-BRINED GRILLED PORK CHOPS

Prep Time: 10 minutes Cooking Time: 15 minutes Serving: 4 servings

Ingredients:

- Four bone-in pork chops (about 1 inch thick)
- 2 cups beer (preferably a lager or ale)
- 1/4 cup soy sauce

- Two tablespoons brown sugar
- Two cloves garlic, minced
- One teaspoon dried thyme
- One teaspoon paprika
- 1/2 teaspoon black pepper
- 1/2 teaspoon salt

Directions:

1. In a large bowl, combine the beer, soy sauce, brown sugar, minced garlic, dried thyme, paprika, black pepper, and salt. Stir well to dissolve the sugar and salt.
2. Place the pork chops in a resealable plastic bag and pour the beer brine over them. Seal the bag, removing as much air as possible. Place the bag in the refrigerator and let the pork chops marinate for at least 2 hours or overnight for best results.
3. Preheat your grill to medium-high heat.
4. Remove the pork chops from the brine and discard the marinade. Pat the chops dry with paper towels.
5. Place the pork chops on the preheated grill and cook for about 6-8 minutes per side, or until the internal temperature reaches 145°F (63°C), using a meat thermometer to check doneness.
6. Remove the pork chops from the grill and let them rest for 5 minutes before serving.
7. Serve the Beer-Brined Grilled Pork Chops hot with your favourite side dishes.

Nutrition Facts (per serving):

- Calories: 300

- Fat: 15g
- Protein: 30g
- Carbohydrates: 8g
- Fibre: 0g
- Sugar: 5g
- Sodium: 800mg

Please note that the nutrition facts are approximate and can vary based on the specific ingredients and quantities used.

Lemon Garlic Shrimp Scampi

Prep Time: 15 minutes Cooking Time: 10 minutes Serving: 4 servings

Ingredients:

- 1 pound (450g) large shrimp, peeled and deveined
- Four tablespoons butter
- Four cloves garlic, minced
- 1/4 cup fresh lemon juice (from about two lemons)
- Zest of 1 lemon
- 1/4 cup dry white wine (optional)
- 1/4 teaspoon red pepper flakes (adjust to taste)
- Salt and pepper, to taste
- Two tablespoons chopped fresh parsley
- Cooked pasta or crusty bread for serving

Directions:

1. In a large skillet, melt the butter over medium heat. Add the minced garlic and sauté for 1-2 minutes until fragrant, being careful not to burn it.

2. Increase the heat to medium-high and add the shrimp to the skillet. Cook for 2-3 minutes on each side until they turn pink and opaque. Remove the shrimp from the skillet and set aside.

3. Pour the lemon juice and white wine (if using) into the skillet. Stir well and let it simmer for 2 minutes to reduce slightly. Add the lemon zest and red pepper flakes, and season with salt and pepper to taste.

4. Return the cooked shrimp to the skillet and toss to coat them with the lemon garlic sauce. Cook for an additional 1-2 minutes to heat the shrimp through.

5. Sprinkle chopped parsley over the shrimp scampi and give it a final stir.

6. Serve the lemon garlic shrimp scampi over cooked pasta or with crusty bread for dipping. Garnish with additional lemon zest and parsley, if desired.

Nutrition Facts (per serving): Calories: 280 Fat: 14g Saturated Fat: 7g Cholesterol: 290mg Sodium: 450mg Carbohydrates: 4g Fiber: 0.5g Sugar: 0.5g Protein: 31g

Note: Nutrition facts may vary depending on the specific ingredients and portion sizes used.

GRILLED BBQ CHICKEN PIZZA

Prep Time: 20 minutes Cooking Time: 15 minutes Servings: 4

Ingredients:

- 1 pound pizza dough (store-bought or homemade)
- 1 cup cooked chicken breast, shredded
- 1/2 cup barbecue sauce

- 1 cup shredded mozzarella cheese
- 1/4 cup red onion, thinly sliced
- Two tablespoons chopped fresh cilantro
- Olive oil for brushing

Directions:

1. Preheat your grill to medium-high heat.
2. On a lightly floured surface, roll out the pizza dough to your desired thickness.
3. Transfer the rolled-out dough onto a pizza peel or baking sheet.
4. In a small bowl, mix the cooked chicken with the barbecue sauce until well coated.
5. Spread the barbecue chicken evenly over the pizza dough.
6. Sprinkle the shredded mozzarella cheese on top of the chicken.
7. Scatter the sliced red onion over the cheese.
8. Sprinkle the chopped cilantro on the pizza as a garnish.
9. Carefully transfer the pizza from the peel or baking sheet onto the preheated grill.
10. Close the grill lid and cook for about 12-15 minutes, or until the crust is golden and the cheese has melted.
11. Once cooked, remove the pizza from the grill using a pizza peel or large spatula.
12. Let the pizza cool for a few minutes, then slice it into wedges and serve.

Nutrition Facts (per serving):

- Calories: 380

- Fat: 12g
- Saturated Fat: 4g
- Cholesterol: 50mg
- Sodium: 890mg
- Carbohydrates: 47g
- Fibre: 2g
- Sugar: 15g
- Protein: 20g

Note: The nutrition facts are approximate and may vary depending on the ingredients used.

KOREAN BBQ BEEF TACOS

Prep Time: 15 minutes Cooking Time: 20 minutes Serving: 4

Ingredients:
- 1 pound beef (such as flank steak or sirloin), thinly sliced
- 1/4 cup soy sauce
- Two tablespoons brown sugar
- Two tablespoons sesame oil
- Two cloves garlic, minced
- One teaspoon grated ginger
- 1 tablespoon rice vinegar
- One tablespoon gochujang (Korean chilli paste)
- Eight small flour tortillas
- 1 cup shredded lettuce
- 1/2 cup thinly sliced red cabbage
- 1/4 cup chopped green onions

- 1/4 cup chopped cilantro
- Lime wedges for serving

Directions:

1. Whisk together the soy sauce, brown sugar, sesame oil, garlic, ginger, rice vinegar, and gochujang in a bowl.
2. Place the sliced beef in a ziplock bag and pour the marinade over it. Seal the bag and let it marinate in the refrigerator for at least 1 hour or overnight for the best flavour.
3. Heat a large skillet or grill pan over medium-high heat. Remove the beef from the marinade and discard the excess marinade.
4. Cook the beef in the hot skillet for about 3-4 minutes per side or until it is browned and cooked to your desired level of doneness.
5. Remove the beef from the skillet and let it rest for a few minutes. Then, thinly slice it into bite-sized pieces.
6. Warm the tortillas in a dry skillet or microwave until soft and pliable.
7. To assemble the tacos, place a spoonful of the beef onto each tortilla. Top with shredded lettuce, sliced red cabbage, green onions, and cilantro.
8. Serve the Korean BBQ beef tacos with lime wedges on the side for squeezing over the tacos.
9. Enjoy your delicious Korean BBQ Beef Tacos!

Nutrition Facts (per serving):

- Calories: 380
- Total Fat: 14g
- Saturated Fat: 4g

- Cholesterol: 70mg
- Sodium: 800mg
- Carbohydrates: 36g
- Fibre: 3g
- Sugar: 7g
- Protein: 27g

Please note that the nutrition facts may vary depending on the specific brands and quantities of ingredients used.

GRILLED WATERMELON SALAD

Prep Time: 15 minutes Cooking Time: 5 minutes Serving: 4 servings

Ingredients:
- Four slices of watermelon, about 1-inch thick
- Two tablespoons olive oil
- Salt and pepper to taste
- 4 cups mixed greens
- 1/2 cup crumbled feta cheese
- 1/4 cup sliced red onion
- 1/4 cup chopped fresh mint
- 1/4 cup balsamic glaze

Directions:
1. Preheat a grill or grill pan to medium-high heat.
2. Brush both sides of the watermelon slices with olive oil and season with salt and pepper.

3. Grill the watermelon slices for about 2-3 minutes per side until grill marks form and the watermelon is slightly softened.
4. Remove the grilled watermelon slices from the grill and let them cool for a few minutes.
5. Cut the grilled watermelon into bite-sized cubes and set aside.
6. In a large bowl, combine the mixed greens, crumbled feta cheese, sliced red onion, and chopped fresh mint.
7. Add the grilled watermelon cubes to the bowl and gently toss everything together.
8. Drizzle the balsamic glaze over the salad and toss again to coat everything evenly.
9. Divide the salad into individual serving plates or bowls.
10. Serve the grilled watermelon salad immediately, and enjoy!

Nutrition Facts (per serving):
- Calories: 180
- Fat: 12g
- Carbohydrates: 14g
- Protein: 5g
- Fibre: 2g

Note: The nutrition facts are approximate and may vary depending on the specific ingredients and quantities used.

PHILLY CHEESESTEAK STUFFED PEPPERS

Prep Time: 15 minutes Cooking Time: 25 minutes Serving: 4

Ingredients:
- Four large bell peppers (any colour)
- One tablespoon olive oil
- One onion, thinly sliced
- One green bell pepper, thinly sliced
- One red bell pepper, thinly sliced
- 8 ounces thinly sliced beef steak (such as ribeye or sirloin)
- Salt and pepper, to taste
- 8 slices provolone cheese

Directions:
1. Preheat your oven to 375°F (190°C). Line a baking sheet with parchment paper.
2. Cut the tops off the bell peppers and remove the seeds and membranes. Place the bell peppers on the prepared baking sheet and set aside.
3. In a large skillet, heat the olive oil over medium heat. Add the onion, green bell pepper, and red bell pepper. Cook, stirring occasionally, until the vegetables are softened, about 5 minutes.
4. Push the vegetables to one side of the skillet and add the sliced beef steak to the other side. Season with salt and pepper. Cook the steak for about 3-4 minutes, stirring occasionally, until browned.
5. Once the steak is cooked, mix it with the sautéed vegetables in the skillet. Cook for an additional 1-2 minutes to ensure the flavours meld together.

6. Spoon the steak and vegetable mixture into the hollowed-out bell peppers. Top each pepper with two slices of provolone cheese.
7. Bake in the preheated oven for 15-20 minutes or until the cheese is melted and bubbly and the peppers are tender.
8. Remove from the oven and let the stuffed peppers cool for a few minutes before serving.
9. Serve the Philly Cheesesteak Stuffed Peppers hot, and enjoy!

Nutrition Facts (per serving):
- Calories: 275
- Fat: 16g
- Carbohydrates: 12g
- Fibre: 3g
- Protein: 20g

Note: Nutrition facts may vary depending on the specific ingredients used.

GRILLED SWEET POTATO FRIES

Prep Time: 10 minutes Cooking Time: 20 minutes Serving: 4 servings

Ingredients:
- 2 large sweet potatoes
- Two tablespoons olive oil
- One teaspoon paprika
- 1 teaspoon garlic powder
- 1/2 teaspoon salt
- 1/4 teaspoon black pepper

- Fresh parsley, chopped (for garnish)

Directions:

1. Preheat your grill to medium-high heat.
2. Peel the sweet potatoes and cut them into long, thin fries, about 1/4-inch thick.
3. In a large bowl, combine the olive oil, paprika, garlic powder, salt, and black pepper. Add the sweet potato fries to the bowl and toss until they are evenly coated with the seasoning mixture.
4. Place the sweet potato fries directly on the grill grates or use a grill basket to prevent them from falling through. Cook for about 10 minutes, flipping occasionally, until the fries are tender and lightly charred.
5. Remove the sweet potato fries from the grill and transfer them to a serving plate. Sprinkle with fresh parsley for added flavour and garnish.
6. Serve the grilled sweet potato fries immediately while they are still hot and crispy. You can enjoy them as a side dish with your favourite dipping sauce or as a delicious snack on their own.

Nutrition Facts (per serving):

- Calories: 150
- Total Fat: 7g
- Saturated Fat: 1g
- Sodium: 305mg
- Total Carbohydrate: 20g
- Dietary Fiber: 4g
- Sugars: 4g

- Protein: 2g

Note: The nutrition facts provided are approximate and may vary based on the specific ingredients used.

BBQ PULLED PORK SANDWICHES

Prep Time: 15 minutes Cooking Time: 8 hours Servings: 6

Ingredients:
- 3 pounds (1.4 kg) of pork shoulder or pork butt
- 1 tablespoon brown sugar
- One tablespoon paprika
- One tablespoon garlic powder
- One tablespoon onion powder
- One teaspoon salt
- 1 teaspoon black pepper
- 1 cup barbecue sauce
- 1/2 cup apple cider vinegar
- Six hamburger buns
- Coleslaw (optional for serving)

Directions:
1. In a small bowl, combine the brown sugar, paprika, garlic powder, onion powder, salt, and black pepper to make a dry rub for the pork.
2. Rub the dry rub mixture all over the pork shoulder, ensuring it is evenly coated.
3. Place the seasoned pork shoulder in a slow cooker or crockpot. Pour the barbecue sauce and apple cider vinegar over the pork.

4. Cover the slow cooker and cook on low heat for 8 hours or until the pork is tender and easily pulls apart with a fork.
5. Once the pork is cooked, remove it from the slow cooker and shred it using two forks.
6. Return the shredded pork to the slow cooker and mix it with the sauce.
7. Toast the hamburger buns until lightly golden.
8. Spoon a generous amount of the pulled pork onto each bun. Top with coleslaw, if desired.
9. Serve the BBQ pulled pork sandwiches warm, and enjoy!

Nutrition Facts (per serving):
- Calories: 480
- Fat: 14g
- Saturated Fat: 5g
- Cholesterol: 150mg
- Sodium: 1050mg
- Carbohydrates: 45g
- Fibre: 2g
- Sugar: 19g
- Protein: 42g

Please note that the nutrition facts are approximate and may vary based on the specific ingredients and brands used.

GRILLED CAESAR SALAD

Prep Time: 15 minutes Cooking Time: 10 minutes Serving: 4

Ingredients:
- Two hearts of romaine lettuce

- Two tablespoons olive oil
- One teaspoon garlic powder
- Salt and pepper, to taste
- 1 cup croutons
- 1/4 cup grated Parmesan cheese
- Caesar dressing (homemade or store-bought)
- Lemon wedges for serving

Directions:

1. Preheat your grill to medium-high heat.
2. Slice the romaine hearts in half lengthwise, keeping the core intact to hold the leaves together.
3. Drizzle the cut sides of the romaine hearts with olive oil and sprinkle with garlic powder, salt, and pepper.
4. Place the romaine hearts, cut side down, on the preheated grill. Cook for about 3-4 minutes, or until you see grill marks and the lettuce begins to wilt slightly.
5. Carefully flip the romaine hearts using tongs, grilling for an additional 2-3 minutes on the other side.
6. Remove the grilled romaine hearts from the grill and transfer them to a serving platter.
7. Sprinkle the croutons over the grilled lettuce halves. Then, generously drizzle Caesar dressing over the top.
8. Finish the salad by sprinkling grated Parmesan cheese evenly over the dressing.
9. Serve the Grilled Caesar Salad immediately, garnished with lemon wedges on the side.

Nutrition Facts (per serving):

- Calories: 180

- Total Fat: 13g
- Saturated Fat: 3g
- Cholesterol: 8mg
- Sodium: 280mg
- Total Carbohydrate: 11g
- Dietary Fiber: 3g
- Sugars: 2g
- Protein: 6g

Note: The nutrition facts may vary depending on the specific brands of ingredients and the homemade or store-bought Caesar dressing used in the recipe.

HONEY SRIRACHA GLAZED CHICKEN SKEWERS

Prep Time: 20 minutes Cooking Time: 15 minutes Serving: 4 servings

Ingredients:
- 1.5 pounds (680g) of boneless, skinless chicken breasts cut into 1-inch cubes
- 1/4 cup honey
- Three tablespoons sriracha sauce
- Two tablespoons soy sauce
- Two tablespoons rice vinegar
- Two cloves garlic, minced
- 1 tablespoon grated fresh ginger
- One tablespoon vegetable oil
- Salt and pepper, to taste

- Bamboo skewers, soaked in water for 30 minutes

Directions:

1. In a medium bowl, whisk together honey, sriracha sauce, soy sauce, rice vinegar, minced garlic, grated ginger, vegetable oil, salt, and pepper. Set aside a small amount of the marinade for brushing the skewers during cooking.
2. Place the chicken cubes in a large resealable plastic bag or a shallow dish. Pour the marinade over the chicken, making sure it is evenly coated. Seal the bag or cover the dish with plastic wrap. Marinate in the refrigerator for at least 1 hour or overnight for more flavour.
3. Preheat the grill to medium-high heat.
4. Thread the marinated chicken onto the soaked bamboo skewers, leaving a little space between each piece.
5. Grease the grill grates lightly with oil to prevent sticking. Place the chicken skewers on the preheated grill and cook for about 6-8 minutes per side, or until the chicken is cooked through and has a nice charred glaze.
6. While grilling, brush the reserved marinade onto the skewers occasionally, turning them to ensure even coating.
7. Remove the chicken skewers from the grill and let them rest for a few minutes before serving.
8. Serve the Honey Sriracha Glazed Chicken Skewers hot with your favourite dipping sauce or a side of steamed rice and grilled vegetables.

Nutrition Facts (per serving): Calories: 280 Total Fat: 6g Saturated Fat: 1g Cholesterol: 90mg Sodium: 740mg Carbohydrate: 19g Fiber: 0.5g Sugar: 17g Protein: 36g

Note: The nutrition facts provided are estimates and may vary depending on the specific ingredients used and the serving size.

GRILLED EGGPLANT PARMESAN

Prep Time: 20 minutes Cooking Time: 30 minutes Serving: 4 servings

Ingredients:

- two large eggplants
- Salt for sprinkling
- Olive oil for brushing
- 2 cups marinara sauce
- 1 cup shredded mozzarella cheese
- 1/2 cup grated Parmesan cheese
- Fresh basil leaves for garnish

Directions:

1. Preheat your grill to medium-high heat.

2. Slice the eggplants into 1/2-inch thick rounds. Sprinkle salt on both sides of each slice and let them sit for about 10 minutes. This will help draw out excess moisture from the eggplant.

3. Rinse the eggplant slices under cold water to remove the salt, then pat them dry with paper towels.

4. Brush both sides of the eggplant slices with olive oil.

5. Grill the eggplant slices for about 2-3 minutes per side until they have grill marks and are tender. Remove them from the grill and set aside.

6. Preheat your oven to 375°F (190°C).

7. In a baking dish, spread a thin layer of marinara sauce on the bottom.

8. Arrange a single layer of grilled eggplant slices on top of the sauce. Sprinkle some mozzarella and Parmesan cheese over the eggplant. Repeat the layers until all the eggplant slices are used, finishing with a layer of cheese on top.

9. Bake in the preheated oven for about 20 minutes or until the cheese is melted and bubbly.

10. Remove from the oven and let it cool for a few minutes. Garnish with fresh basil leaves before serving.

Nutrition Facts (per serving):

- Calories: 230
- Total Fat: 13g
- Saturated Fat: 5g
- Cholesterol: 25mg
- Sodium: 780mg
- Total Carbohydrate: 18g
- Dietary Fiber: 7g
- Sugars: 11g
- Protein: 12g

Note: The nutrition facts provided are approximate values and may vary based on the specific ingredients used and serving size.

Bacon-Wrapped Scallops

Prep Time: 15 minutes Cooking Time: 15 minutes Serving: 4

Ingredients:

- 12 large sea scallops
- 12 slices of bacon
- 2 tablespoons olive oil

- Salt and pepper, to taste
- one tablespoon of fresh parsley, chopped (for garnish)
- Lemon wedges for serving

Directions:

1. Preheat the oven to 400°F (200°C). Line a baking sheet with aluminium foil and set aside.

2. Rinse the scallops under cold water and pat them dry with paper towels. Season with salt and pepper.

3. Take each slice of bacon and wrap it around a scallop, securing it with a toothpick. Repeat with the remaining scallops and bacon.

4. Heat the olive oil in a large skillet over medium heat. Place the bacon-wrapped scallops in the skillet and cook for 2-3 minutes on each side until the bacon is crispy and cooked through.

5. Transfer the cooked scallops to the prepared baking sheet and place them in the preheated oven. Bake for 5-7 minutes until the scallops are cooked through and tender.

6. Remove the toothpicks from the scallops before serving. Garnish with fresh parsley.

7. Serve the bacon-wrapped scallops hot with lemon wedges on the side for squeezing over the scallops. They can be enjoyed as an appetizer or a main course.

Nutrition Facts:

- Serving Size: 3 bacon-wrapped scallops
- Calories: 250
- Total Fat: 15g
- Saturated Fat: 4g
- Cholesterol: 55mg

- Sodium: 600mg
- Total Carbohydrate: 3g
- Protein: 24g

Note: Nutritional values are approximate and may vary depending on the ingredients used.

GRILLED BRATWURST WITH SAUERKRAUT

Prep Time: 10 minutes Cooking Time: 20 minutes Serving: 4 servings

Ingredients:

- 4 bratwurst sausages
- four bratwurst buns
- 1 cup sauerkraut
- one tablespoon of vegetable oil
- one tablespoon of butter
- Mustard (optional)
- Salt and pepper to taste

Directions:

1. Preheat your grill to medium-high heat.

2. heat the vegetable oil and butter over medium heat in a skillet. Add the sauerkraut and cook for about 5 minutes, stirring occasionally, until heated through. Season with salt and pepper to taste. Set aside.

3. Place the bratwurst sausages on the grill and cook for about 10-12 minutes, turning occasionally, until they are browned and cooked through.

4. While the sausages are grilling, lightly toast the bratwurst buns on the grill or in a toaster.

5. Once the bratwurst sausages are cooked, remove them from the grill and let them rest for a few minutes.

6. To assemble, place a grilled bratwurst sausage in each bun. Top with a generous portion of sauerkraut. Add mustard if desired.

7. Serve the grilled bratwurst with sauerkraut immediately while still warm. Enjoy!

Nutrition Facts (per serving):

- Calories: 400
- Fat: 25g
- Saturated Fat: 9g
- Cholesterol: 60mg
- Sodium: 950mg
- Carbohydrates: 30g
- Fiber: 3g
- Sugar: 3g
- Protein: 15g

Note: The nutrition facts are approximate and may vary depending on the ingredients used.

GRILLED TERIYAKI SALMON

Prep Time: 10 minutes Cooking Time: 15 minutes Serving: 4 servings

Ingredients:

- four salmon fillets
- 1/2 cup teriyaki sauce

- two tablespoons of honey
- two tablespoons of soy sauce
- two cloves garlic, minced
- one tablespoon of ginger, grated
- one tablespoon of sesame oil
- one tablespoon of vegetable oil
- one green onion, chopped (for garnish)
- Sesame seeds (for garnish)

Directions:

1. In a bowl, whisk together teriyaki sauce, honey, soy sauce, minced garlic, grated ginger, sesame oil, and vegetable oil. This will be your marinade.

2. Place the salmon fillets in a shallow dish or a ziplock bag, and pour the marinade over them. Make sure the salmon is coated evenly. Allow it to marinate for at least 30 minutes or overnight in the refrigerator.

3. Preheat your grill to medium-high heat. Make sure the grill grates are clean and lightly oiled to prevent sticking.

4. Remove the salmon fillets from the marinade, shaking off any excess marinade, and place them on the grill, skin side down. Reserve the marinade for basting.

5. Grill the salmon for about 5-7 minutes on each side, basting occasionally with the reserved marinade until the salmon is cooked through and flakes easily with a fork. Be careful not to overcook the salmon.

6. Once cooked, remove the salmon from the grill and transfer it to a serving plate.

7. Garnish the grilled teriyaki salmon with chopped green onions and sesame seeds.

8. Serve hot with steamed rice and your choice of vegetables.

Nutrition Facts (per serving):

- Calories: 350
- Total Fat: 17g
- Saturated Fat: 3g
- Cholesterol: 85mg
- Sodium: 950mg
- Carbohydrate: 18g
- Fiber: 0.5g
- Sugar: 15g
- Protein: 32g

Note: The nutrition facts are approximate and may vary based on the specific ingredients used.

SOUTHWEST CHICKEN QUESADILLAS

Prep Time: 15 minutes Cooking Time: 20 minutes Serving: 4

Ingredients:

- 2 cups cooked chicken breast, shredded
- 1 cup black beans, rinsed and drained
- 1 cup corn kernels, fresh or frozen
- one red bell pepper, diced
- one small red onion, diced
- two cloves garlic, minced
- one teaspoon of ground cumin

- one teaspoon of chili powder
- 1/2 teaspoon smoked paprika
- Salt and pepper to taste
- one tablespoon of olive oil
- four large flour tortillas
- 2 cups shredded Monterey Jack cheese
- 1/4 cup chopped fresh cilantro
- Sour cream, salsa, and guacamole for serving

Directions:

1. heat the olive oil over medium heat in a large skillet. Add the diced onion, garlic, red bell pepper, corn, and black beans. Cook for 5-7 minutes until the vegetables are tender.

2. Add the shredded chicken to the skillet and season with cumin, chilli powder, smoked paprika, salt, and pepper. Stir well to combine and cook for 3-4 minutes to heat through.

3. Preheat a separate large skillet or griddle over medium heat. Place one flour tortilla on the skillet and sprinkle with a quarter of the shredded cheese. Spoon a quarter of the chicken and vegetable mixture on one side of the tortilla. Sprinkle with some chopped cilantro. Fold the tortilla in half to create a quesadilla.

4. Cook the quesadilla for 2-3 minutes on each side until the tortilla is golden brown and the cheese is melted. Remove from the skillet and repeat the process with the remaining tortillas and filling.

5. Cut each quesadilla into wedges and serve hot with sour cream, salsa, and guacamole on the side.

Nutrition Facts (per serving):

- Calories: 450

- Fat: 20g
- Carbohydrates: 38g
- Fiber: 6g
- Protein: 30g

Note: The nutrition facts are approximate and may vary depending on the ingredients used.

GRILLED VEGETABLE PANINI

Prep Time: 15 minutes Cooking Time: 20 minutes Serving: 2 paninis

Ingredients:
- one zucchini, sliced
- one red bell pepper, sliced
- one yellow bell pepper, sliced
- one small eggplant, sliced
- one red onion, sliced
- four slices of crusty bread (such as ciabatta or baguette)
- four tablespoons of pesto sauce
- four slices of provolone cheese
- Salt and pepper to taste
- Olive oil for grilling

Directions:

1. Preheat a grill or stovetop grill pan over medium-high heat.

2. In a large bowl, toss the zucchini, red bell pepper, yellow bell pepper, eggplant, and red onion with olive oil, salt, and pepper.

3. Place the vegetables on the grill and cook for about 4-5 minutes per side until they are tender and lightly charred. Remove from the grill and set aside.

4. Take each slice of bread and spread one tablespoon of pesto sauce on one side of each slice.

5. Layer the grilled vegetables on two slices of bread. Top each with two slices of provolone cheese.

6. Place the remaining bread slices on top to make sandwiches, with the pesto side facing inward.

7. Heat a panini press or a stovetop grill pan over medium heat. If using a stovetop grill pan, place a heavy pan or skillet on top of the sandwiches to press them down.

8. Grill the paninis for about 3-4 minutes on each side until the cheese has melted and the bread is toasted and crispy.

9. Remove the paninis from the grill, let them cool for a minute, then slice them in half.

10. Serve the Grilled Vegetable Panini warm, and enjoy!

Nutrition Facts (per serving):

- Calories: 380
- Total Fat: 18g
- Saturated Fat: 7g
- Cholesterol: 25mg
- Sodium: 780mg
- Carbohydrates: 41g
- Fiber: 7g
- Sugar: 11g
- Protein: 16g

Please note that the nutrition facts provided are estimated and may vary based on the specific ingredients used and serving size.

GRILLED SHRIMP AND PINEAPPLE SKEWERS

Prep Time: 20 minutes Cooking Time: 10 minutes Serving: 4 servings

Ingredients:

- 1 pound (450g) large shrimp, peeled and deveined
- one small pineapple, peeled, cored, and cut into chunks
- two tablespoons of olive oil
- two tablespoons of soy sauce
- two tablespoons of honey
- one tablespoon of lime juice
- two cloves garlic, minced
- one teaspoon of grated fresh ginger
- Salt and pepper, to taste
- Wooden or metal skewers

Directions:

1. In a large bowl, whisk together the olive oil, soy sauce, honey, lime juice, minced garlic, grated ginger, salt, and pepper to make the marinade.

2. Add the shrimp to the marinade and toss to coat. Allow the shrimp to marinate for about 10 minutes.

3. Preheat your grill to medium-high heat.

4. Thread the marinated shrimp and pineapple chunks onto skewers, alternating between shrimp and pineapple.

5. Place the skewers on the preheated grill and cook for about 4-5 minutes per side, or until the shrimp are pink and opaque and the pineapple has grill marks.

6. Remove the skewers from the grill and serve hot.

Nutrition Facts (per serving):

- Calories: 230
- Total Fat: 7g
- Saturated Fat: 1g
- Cholesterol: 165mg
- Sodium: 720mg
- Carbohydrates: 24g
- Fiber: 2g
- Sugar: 18g
- Protein: 18g

Enjoy your Grilled Shrimp and Pineapple Skewers!

BBQ BACON-WRAPPED MEATLOAF

Prep Time: 20 minutes Cooking Time: 1-hour Servings: 6

Ingredients:

- 1.5 pounds of ground beef
- 1/2 cup breadcrumbs
- 1/2 cup diced onion
- 1/4 cup diced green bell pepper
- two cloves garlic, minced
- 1/4 cup ketchup
- two tablespoons of Worcestershire sauce

- one tablespoon of Dijon mustard
- one teaspoon of salt
- 1/2 teaspoon black pepper
- six slices of bacon
- 1/2 cup barbecue sauce

Directions:

1. Preheat your oven to 375°F (190°C) and line a baking sheet with foil.

2. In a large bowl, combine the ground beef, breadcrumbs, onion, green bell pepper, garlic, ketchup, Worcestershire sauce, Dijon mustard, salt, and black pepper. Mix well until all the ingredients are evenly incorporated.

3. Shape the meat mixture into a loaf shape and place it on the prepared baking sheet.

4. Lay the bacon slices over the meatloaf, tucking the ends underneath. You can create a lattice pattern with the bacon for an attractive presentation if desired.

5. Brush the barbecue sauce over the bacon-wrapped meatloaf, covering it completely.

6. Place the baking sheet in the preheated oven and bake for 1 hour or until the meatloaf is cooked and the bacon is crispy.

7. Remove the meatloaf from the oven and let it rest for 5-10 minutes before slicing.

8. Serve the BBQ Bacon-Wrapped Meatloaf slices with additional barbecue sauce on the side if desired.

Nutrition Facts (per serving): Calories: 365 Total Fat: 21g
- Saturated Fat: 7g

- Trans Fat: 1g Cholesterol: 97mg Sodium: 948mg Total Carbohydrate: 17g
- Dietary Fiber: 1g
- Sugars: 9g Protein: 25g

Please note that the nutrition facts are approximate and may vary depending on the specific ingredients and brands used.

GRILLED CORN AND BLACK BEAN SALAD

Prep Time: 15 minutes Cooking Time: 15 minutes Servings: 4

Ingredients:

- four ears of corn, husks removed
- one can (15 ounces) of black beans, rinsed and drained
- one red bell pepper, diced
- one small red onion, finely chopped
- one jalapeno pepper, seeded and minced
- 1/4 cup fresh cilantro, chopped
- two tablespoons of olive oil
- Juice of 1 lime
- one teaspoon of ground cumin
- Salt and pepper to taste

Directions:

1. Preheat a grill or grill pan over medium-high heat.

2. Grill the corn for about 10-12 minutes, turning occasionally, until it is slightly charred. Remove from the grill and let it cool slightly.

3. Using a sharp knife, cut the kernels off the cobs and transfer them to a large bowl.

4. Add the black beans, red bell pepper, red onion, jalapeno pepper, and cilantro to the bowl with the corn.

5. In a small bowl, whisk together the olive oil, lime juice, cumin, salt, and pepper.

6. Pour the dressing over the salad ingredients and toss well to combine.

7. Adjust the seasoning if needed.

8. Let the salad sit for about 10 minutes to allow the flavours to meld together.

9. Serve the grilled corn and black bean salad at room temperature.

Nutrition Facts (per serving): Calories: 220 Fat: 7g Carbohydrates: 35g Fiber: 9g Protein: 9g

Note: Nutrition facts may vary depending on the specific ingredients and brands used.

GARLIC BUTTER GRILLED LOBSTER TAILS

Prep Time: 15 minutes Cooking Time: 10 minutes Serving: 2

Ingredients:
- two lobster tails
- four tablespoons unsalted butter, melted
- four cloves garlic, minced
- two tablespoons fresh parsley, chopped
- 1/2 teaspoon salt
- 1/4 teaspoon black pepper
- Lemon wedges for serving

Directions:

1. Preheat the grill to medium-high heat.

2. Using kitchen shears, carefully cut along the top of each lobster tail shell to expose the meat. Gently lift the meat out of the shell, keeping it attached at the base. Place the lobster tails on a plate.

3. In a small bowl, combine the melted butter, minced garlic, chopped parsley, salt, and black pepper. Mix well.

4. Brush the garlic butter mixture over the lobster meat, ensuring it is evenly coated.

5. Place the lobster tails on the preheated grill, meat side down. Cook for about 4-5 minutes.

6. Flip the lobster tails and continue grilling for another 4-5 minutes or until the meat is opaque and cooked through. Baste with the remaining garlic butter mixture while grilling.

7. Remove the lobster tails from the grill and transfer them to a serving platter. Let them rest for a couple of minutes.

8. Serve the grilled lobster tails with lemon wedges on the side for squeezing over the meat. You can also garnish with additional chopped parsley if desired.

Nutrition Facts (per serving): Calories: 280 Fat: 18g Saturated Fat: 10g Cholesterol: 150mg Sodium: 680mg Carbohydrates: 3g Fiber: 0g Sugar: 0g Protein: 27g

Enjoy your delicious Garlic Butter Grilled Lobster Tails!

Teriyaki Glazed Pork Tenderloin

Prep Time: 10 minutes Cooking Time: 25 minutes Serving: 4

Ingredients:

- 1 ½ pounds of pork tenderloin
- ¼ cup soy sauce

- ¼ cup mirin (Japanese rice wine)
- two tablespoons brown sugar
- two tablespoons of honey
- two tablespoons of rice vinegar
- two garlic cloves minced
- one teaspoon of grated fresh ginger
- one tablespoon of vegetable oil
- Sesame seeds for garnish
- Sliced green onions for garnish

Directions:

1. Preheat your oven to 425°F (220°C).

2. In a small bowl, whisk together the soy sauce, mirin, brown sugar, honey, rice vinegar, minced garlic, and grated ginger to make the teriyaki sauce.

3. Heat the vegetable oil in an oven-safe skillet over medium-high heat.

4. Season the pork tenderloin with salt and pepper, then sear it in the hot skillet until browned on all sides, about 2 minutes per side.

5. Pour the teriyaki sauce over the seared pork tenderloin, ensuring it's evenly coated.

6. Transfer the skillet to the preheated oven and roast for about 20-25 minutes, or until the internal temperature of the pork reaches 145°F (63°C).

7. Baste the pork with the teriyaki sauce occasionally while it cooks.

8. Once cooked, remove the skillet from the oven and let the pork rest for 5 minutes before slicing.

9. Slice the pork tenderloin into ½-inch thick slices and arrange on a serving platter.

10. Garnish with sesame seeds and sliced green onions.

11. Serve the Teriyaki Glazed Pork Tenderloin with steamed rice or your choice of side dishes.

Nutrition Facts (per serving):

- Calories: 280
- Total Fat: 7g
- Saturated Fat: 2g
- Cholesterol: 110mg
- Sodium: 700mg
- Total Carbohydrate: 15g
- Dietary Fiber: 0g
- Sugars: 13g
- Protein: 36g

Note: The nutrition facts are approximate and may vary depending on the specific ingredients and quantities used.

GRILLED CAPRESE SANDWICH

Prep Time: 10 minutes Cooking Time: 10 minutes Serving: 2 sandwiches

Ingredients:

- four slices of Italian bread
- 4 tablespoons of basil pesto
- one large tomato, sliced
- 8 ounces of fresh mozzarella cheese, sliced

- Fresh basil leaves
- Salt and pepper, to taste
- Olive oil for grilling

Directions:

1. Preheat a grill pan or skillet over medium heat.
2. Spread one tablespoon of basil pesto on each slice of bread.
3. Layer tomato slices on two slices of bread.
4. Add fresh mozzarella slices on top of the tomatoes.
5. Place a few basil leaves on the cheese and sprinkle with salt and pepper.
6. Cover the sandwiches with the remaining slices of bread, pesto side down.
7. Lightly brush the outer sides of the sandwiches with olive oil.
8. Place the sandwiches on the preheated grill pan or skillet.
9. Grill for about 3-4 minutes on each side or until the bread is toasted and the cheese has melted.
10. Remove the sandwiches from the heat and let them cool for a minute.
11. Cut the sandwiches in half diagonally and serve.

Nutrition Facts (per serving):

- Calories: 420
- Fat: 23g
- Saturated Fat: 11g
- Cholesterol: 60mg
- Sodium: 650mg
- Carbohydrates: 31g
- Fiber: 3g

- Sugar: 4g
- Protein: 23g

Note: The nutrition facts are approximate and may vary depending on the specific brands of ingredients used.

LEMON HERB GRILLED CHICKEN

Prep Time: 10 minutes Cooking Time: 15 minutes Serving: 4 servings

Ingredients:

- four boneless, skinless chicken breasts
- two lemons, juiced and zested
- three tablespoons of olive oil
- three cloves garlic, minced
- two tablespoons fresh parsley, chopped
- one tablespoon of fresh rosemary, chopped
- one tablespoon of fresh thyme leaves
- Salt and pepper to taste

Directions:

1. In a small bowl, combine the lemon juice, lemon zest, olive oil, minced garlic, parsley, rosemary, thyme, salt, and pepper. Mix well to create the marinade.

2. Place the chicken breasts in a shallow dish or a resealable plastic bag and pour the marinade over them. Make sure the chicken is well coated. Let it marinate in the refrigerator for at least 30 minutes or overnight for more flavour.

3. Preheat the grill to medium-high heat.

4. Remove the chicken breasts from the marinade and discard any excess marinade.

5. Grill the chicken for about 6-8 minutes per side, or until the internal temperature reaches 165°F (74°C) and the chicken is cooked through. Cooking time may vary depending on the thickness of the chicken breasts.

6. Once cooked, remove the chicken from the grill and let it rest for a few minutes.

7. Serve the Lemon Herb Grilled Chicken with a squeeze of fresh lemon juice on top. You can also garnish with additional herbs if desired.

Nutrition Facts (per serving):

- Calories: 250
- Fat: 10g
- Carbohydrates: 2g
- Protein: 35g
- Fiber: 0.5g

Enjoy your delicious Lemon Herb Grilled Chicken!

GRILLED TERIYAKI VEGGIE KABOBS

Prep Time: 20 minutes Cooking Time: 15 minutes Serving: 4

Ingredients:

- two bell peppers (any colour), cut into chunks
- one zucchini, sliced
- one yellow squash, sliced
- one red onion, cut into chunks
- eight cherry tomatoes

- 1 cup button mushrooms
- 1/4 cup teriyaki sauce
- two tablespoons of soy sauce
- two tablespoons of honey
- two tablespoons of vegetable oil
- Salt and pepper to taste
- Wooden or metal skewers

Directions:

1. Preheat your grill to medium-high heat.

2. In a small bowl, whisk together the teriyaki sauce, soy sauce, honey, vegetable oil, salt, and pepper to make the marinade.

3. Thread the vegetables onto skewers, alternating between the different veggies. Make sure to leave a little space between each piece for even cooking.

4. Place the assembled kabobs on a baking sheet or tray and brush them generously with the teriyaki marinade, making sure to coat all sides.

5. Once the grill is hot, place the kabobs on the grill grates and close the lid. Cook for about 10-15 minutes, turning occasionally and basting with the marinade. The vegetables should be tender and slightly charred.

6. Remove the kabobs from the grill and let them cool for a few minutes. Serve hot with any remaining teriyaki sauce on the side for dipping.

Nutrition Facts (per serving):

- Calories: 150
- Fat: 7g
- Carbohydrates: 21g

- Fiber: 5g
- Protein: 4g

Note: You can customize this recipe by adding other vegetables of your choice, like mushrooms, cherry tomatoes, or eggplant. You can also add tofu or tempeh for extra protein. Enjoy your grilled teriyaki veggie kabobs!

BBQ PULLED CHICKEN TACOS

Prep Time: 15 minutes Cooking Time: 4 hours Servings: 4

Ingredients:

- 1.5 pounds (680g) of boneless, skinless chicken breasts
- 1 cup barbecue sauce
- 1/2 cup chicken broth
- two tablespoons brown sugar
- one tablespoon of apple cider vinegar
- one teaspoon of smoked paprika
- 1/2 teaspoon garlic powder
- 1/2 teaspoon onion powder
- Salt and pepper, to taste
- eight small flour tortillas
- Shredded lettuce
- Diced tomatoes
- Sliced red onions
- Chopped cilantro
- Lime wedges for serving

Directions:

1. In a slow cooker, combine barbecue sauce, chicken broth, brown sugar, apple cider vinegar, smoked paprika, garlic powder, onion powder, salt, and pepper. Mix well to combine.

2. Add the chicken breasts to the slow cooker and coat them with the sauce mixture.

3. Cover the slow cooker and cook on low heat for 4 hours or until the chicken is tender and easily shreds with a fork.

4. Once the chicken is cooked, remove it from the slow cooker and shred it using two forks.

5. Meanwhile, heat the flour tortillas in a dry skillet over medium heat until warm and pliable.

6. To assemble the tacos, place a generous amount of the pulled chicken onto each tortilla.

7. Top the chicken with shredded lettuce, diced tomatoes, sliced red onions, and chopped cilantro.

8. Squeeze fresh lime juice over the tacos for added flavour.

9. Serve the BBQ Pulled Chicken Tacos immediately and enjoy!

Nutrition Facts (per serving):

- Calories: 420
- Fat: 8g
- Carbohydrates: 57g
- Protein: 30g
- Fiber: 3g

Note: The nutrition facts may vary depending on the specific brands and quantities of ingredients used.

GRILLED ROMAINE LETTUCE WITH PARMESAN DRESSING

Prep Time: 10 minutes Cooking Time: 10 minutes Serving: 4 servings

Ingredients:

- two heads of romaine lettuce
- two tablespoons of olive oil
- Salt and pepper, to taste
- 1/2 cup grated Parmesan cheese
- 1/4 cup mayonnaise
- 1/4 cup Greek yogurt
- two tablespoons of lemon juice
- one garlic clove, minced
- one teaspoon of Dijon mustard
- 1/4 teaspoon Worcestershire sauce

Directions:

1. Preheat your grill to medium-high heat.

2. Cut the romaine lettuce heads in half lengthwise, keeping the core intact to hold the leaves together.

3. Brush the cut sides of the romaine lettuce with olive oil and season with salt and pepper.

4. Place the romaine lettuce halves on the grill, cut side down. Cook for about 2-3 minutes until grill marks appear and the lettuce is slightly charred.

5. Flip the lettuce halves and grill for another 2-3 minutes.

6. Remove the grilled romaine lettuce from the grill and set aside.

7. In a small bowl, combine the grated Parmesan cheese, mayonnaise, Greek yoghurt, lemon juice, minced garlic, Dijon

mustard, and Worcestershire sauce. Mix well until the dressing is smooth and creamy.

8. Drizzle the Parmesan dressing over the grilled romaine lettuce halves.

9. Serve the grilled romaine lettuce with Parmesan dressing immediately.

Nutrition Facts:

- Serving Size: 1/2 grilled romaine lettuce with dressing
- Calories: 180
- Total Fat: 14g
- Saturated Fat: 4g
- Cholesterol: 20mg
- Sodium: 350mg
- Total Carbohydrate: 7g
- Dietary Fiber: 3g
- Sugars: 2g
- Protein: 8g

Note: The nutrition facts are approximate and may vary depending on the specific ingredients and brands used.

KOREAN BBQ BEEF TACOS

Prep Time: 20 minutes Cooking Time: 20 minutes Serving: 4

Ingredients:

- 1 pound beef sirloin, thinly sliced
- 1/4 cup soy sauce
- two tablespoons brown sugar

- two tablespoons of sesame oil
- two cloves garlic, minced
- one teaspoon of ginger, grated
- one tablespoon of rice vinegar
- one tablespoon gochujang (Korean red chilli paste)
- one tablespoon of vegetable oil
- eight small flour tortillas
- 1 cup shredded lettuce
- 1/2 cup thinly sliced carrots
- 1/4 cup chopped green onions
- 1/4 cup chopped fresh cilantro
- Lime wedges for serving

Directions:

1. In a bowl, combine soy sauce, brown sugar, sesame oil, minced garlic, grated ginger, rice vinegar, and gochujang. Whisk well to make the marinade.

2. Place the thinly sliced beef in a ziplock bag or a shallow dish. Pour the marinade over the beef, ensuring it is evenly coated. Marinate for at least 15 minutes, or refrigerate overnight for enhanced flavour.

3. Heat vegetable oil in a large skillet or grill pan over medium-high heat. Remove the beef from the marinade, allowing any excess marinade to drip off. Reserve the marinade for later.

4. Cook the beef slices in the hot skillet for about 2-3 minutes per side or until they are browned and cooked to your desired doneness. Transfer the cooked beef to a plate and set aside.

5. In the same skillet, pour the reserved marinade and bring it to a boil. Reduce the heat to low and let it simmer for 5 minutes or until the sauce thickens slightly.

6. Warm the flour tortillas in a dry skillet or oven until they are soft and pliable.

7. To assemble the tacos, place a small amount of shredded lettuce on each tortilla. Top with a few slices of cooked beef, followed by sliced carrots, chopped green onions, and fresh cilantro. Drizzle the simmered marinade sauce over the taco fillings.

8. Serve the Korean BBQ Beef Tacos with lime wedges on the side for squeezing over the tacos.

Nutrition Facts (per serving): Calories: 380 Total Fat: 14g Saturated Fat: 3g Cholesterol: 55mg Sodium: 900mg Total Carbohydrate: 36g Dietary Fiber: 3g Sugar: 9g Protein: 27g

Note: The nutrition facts are approximate and may vary based on the specific ingredients used.

GRILLED SWEET AND SPICY CHICKEN WINGS

Prep Time: 10 minutes Cooking Time: 20 minutes Servings: 4

Ingredients:
- 2 pounds of chicken wings
- 1/4 cup soy sauce
- 1/4 cup honey
- Two tablespoons of hot sauce
- Two tablespoons of vegetable oil

- Two cloves garlic, minced
- One teaspoon of ground ginger
- Salt and pepper, to taste
- Chopped green onions for garnish
- Sesame seeds, for garnish

Directions:

1. In a large bowl, combine the soy sauce, honey, hot sauce, vegetable oil, minced garlic, ground ginger, salt, and pepper. Mix well to create the marinade.
2. Add the chicken wings to the bowl and toss them in the marinade until they are well coated. Allow the wings to marinate for at least 30 minutes or up to overnight in the refrigerator for maximum flavour.
3. Preheat your grill to medium-high heat.
4. Remove the chicken wings from the marinade and discard any excess marinade. Place the wings on the preheated grill and cook for about 10 minutes on each side or until they are cooked through and have nice grill marks.
5. While the wings are cooking, you can brush them with the leftover marinade to add flavour.
6. Once the wings are cooked, remove them from the grill and transfer them to a serving platter. Garnish with chopped green onions and sesame seeds.
7. Serve the grilled sweet and spicy chicken wings hot as an appetizer or as part of a main course. They pair well with a side of rice or a fresh salad.

Nutrition Facts (per serving):

- Calories: 350

- Fat: 18g
- Saturated Fat: 4g
- Cholesterol: 105mg
- Sodium: 830mg
- Carbohydrates: 18g
- Fibre: 0g
- Sugar: 16g
- Protein: 28g

Note: The nutrition facts provided are approximate and may vary depending on the specific ingredients used.

GARLIC BUTTER GRILLED SHRIMP

Prep Time: 15 minutes Cooking Time: 6 minutes Serving: 4 servings

Ingredients:
- 1 pound large shrimp, peeled and deveined
- Four cloves garlic, minced
- Four tablespoons unsalted butter melted
- Two tablespoons fresh parsley chopped
- One tablespoon of lemon juice
- Salt and black pepper to taste
- Skewers (if using wooden skewers, soak them in water for 30 minutes before grilling)

Directions:
1. In a bowl, combine the minced garlic, melted butter, chopped parsley, lemon juice, salt, and black pepper. Mix well to make the garlic butter marinade.

2. Add the peeled and deveined shrimp to the marinade and toss until the shrimp are evenly coated. Let the shrimp marinate for about 10 minutes.
3. Preheat your grill to medium-high heat.
4. Thread the marinated shrimp onto skewers if using.
5. Place the shrimp skewers on the preheated grill and cook for approximately 3 minutes per side or until the shrimp turn pink and opaque. Be careful not to overcook them, as they can become rubbery.
6. Once cooked, remove the shrimp from the grill and transfer them to a serving platter.
7. Serve the garlic butter grilled shrimp immediately, garnished with additional chopped parsley if desired.

Nutrition Facts (per serving):
- Calories: 240
- Total Fat: 15g
- Saturated Fat: 8g
- Cholesterol: 240mg
- Sodium: 320mg
- Total Carbohydrate: 2g
- Dietary Fiber: 0g
- Sugars: 0g
- Protein: 24g

Note: Nutrition facts may vary depending on the specific ingredients and quantities used.

GRILLED RATATOUILLE

Prep Time: 15 minutes Cooking Time: 25 minutes Serving: 4 servings

Ingredients:

- One eggplant, sliced into 1/2-inch rounds
- Two zucchinis, sliced into 1/2-inch rounds
- One red bell pepper, seeded and sliced
- One yellow bell pepper, seeded and sliced
- One large red onion, sliced
- Three tablespoons olive oil
- Three cloves garlic, minced
- Two tablespoons of balsamic vinegar
- One teaspoon of dried thyme
- Salt and pepper to taste
- Fresh basil leaves for garnish

Directions:

1. Preheat a grill to medium-high heat.
2. In a large bowl, toss the eggplant, zucchini, red bell pepper, yellow bell pepper, and red onion with olive oil, minced garlic, balsamic vinegar, dried thyme, salt, and pepper. Make sure the vegetables are well coated.
3. Place the vegetables on the preheated grill and cook for about 10-12 minutes, or until they are tender and slightly charred, turning them occasionally to ensure even cooking.
4. Remove the grilled vegetables from the heat and let them cool slightly. Cut them into bite-sized pieces and transfer them to a serving dish.
5. Garnish with fresh basil leaves and drizzle with extra olive oil, if desired.

6. Serve the Grilled Ratatouille warm or at room temperature as a side dish or main course.

Nutrition Facts (per serving):

- Calories: 150
- Fat: 10g
- Carbohydrates: 14g
- Fibre: 6g
- Protein: 2g
- Vitamin A: 25% DV
- Vitamin C: 90% DV
- Iron: 4% DV
- Calcium: 2% DV

Note: The nutrition facts are approximate and may vary based on the specific ingredients used.

KOREAN BBQ CHICKEN

Prep Time: 10 minutes Cooking Time: 20 minutes Serving: 4 servings

Ingredients:

- Four boneless, skinless chicken breasts
- 1/4 cup soy sauce
- 1/4 cup honey
- Two tablespoons brown sugar
- 2 tablespoons sesame oil
- Two tablespoons of rice vinegar
- Four cloves garlic, minced

- One tablespoon of grated fresh ginger
- Two tablespoons gochujang (Korean red chilli paste)
- Two green onions, thinly sliced
- Sesame seeds, for garnish
- Steamed rice for serving

Directions:

1. In a bowl, whisk together soy sauce, honey, brown sugar, sesame oil, rice vinegar, minced garlic, grated ginger, and gochujang to make the marinade.
2. Place the chicken breasts in a shallow dish and pour the marinade over them, ensuring they are well coated. Marinate for at least 30 minutes or up to 24 hours for maximum flavour.
3. Preheat your grill or grill pan over medium-high heat. Remove the chicken from the marinade, allowing any excess to drip off.
4. Grill the chicken for about 8-10 minutes per side or until the internal temperature reaches 165°F (74°C). Baste with the remaining marinade during grilling.
5. Once cooked, remove the chicken from the grill and let it rest for a few minutes. Slice the chicken into thin strips.
6. Serve the Korean BBQ chicken over steamed rice and garnish with sliced green onions and sesame seeds.

Nutrition Facts (per serving):

- Calories: 300
- Total Fat: 7g
- Saturated Fat: 1.5g
- Cholesterol: 85mg

- Sodium: 800mg
- Total Carbohydrate: 23g
- Dietary Fiber: 1g
- Sugars: 19g
- Protein: 34g

Note: The nutrition facts are approximate and may vary based on the specific ingredients used.

GRILLED TERIYAKI BEEF SKEWERS

Prep Time: 15 minutes Cooking Time: 15 minutes Serving: 4 servings

Ingredients:

- 1 pound beef sirloin, cut into 1-inch cubes
- 1/4 cup soy sauce
- Two tablespoons honey
- Two tablespoons of rice vinegar
- Two tablespoons of vegetable oil
- Two cloves garlic, minced
- One teaspoon of grated ginger
- 1/4 teaspoon red pepper flakes (optional)
- Wooden skewers, soaked in water for 30 minutes

Directions:

1. In a bowl, combine soy sauce, honey, rice vinegar, vegetable oil, minced garlic, grated ginger, and red pepper flakes (if desired). Mix well to make the teriyaki marinade.

2. Place the beef cubes in a ziplock bag or a shallow dish. Pour the teriyaki marinade over the beef, ensuring it is fully coated. Marinate the beef for at least 1 hour or overnight in the refrigerator for maximum flavour.
3. Preheat your grill to medium-high heat.
4. Thread the marinated beef onto the soaked wooden skewers, leaving a little space between each piece.
5. Grill the skewers for 2-3 minutes per side or until the beef is cooked to your desired doneness. Rotate the skewers occasionally to ensure even cooking and to prevent burning.
6. Once the beef is cooked, remove the skewers from the grill and let them rest for a few minutes.
7. Serve the grilled teriyaki beef skewers as a main course or appetizer. They go well with steamed rice, stir-fried vegetables, or a fresh salad.

Nutrition Facts (per serving):
- Calories: 280
- Fat: 16g
- Saturated Fat: 5g
- Cholesterol: 75mg
- Sodium: 850mg
- Carbohydrates: 10g
- Fibre: 0g
- Sugar: 9g
- Protein: 24g
- Vitamin D: 0mcg
- Calcium: 20mg
- Iron: 3mg

- Potassium: 390mg

Note: Nutrition facts are approximate and may vary depending on the ingredients used.

BBQ BACON-WRAPPED STUFFED JALAPENOS

Prep Time: 20 minutes Cooking Time: 25 minutes Serving: 8 jalapeno poppers

Ingredients:

- Eight large jalapeno peppers
- Eight slices of bacon
- 1 cup cream cheese, softened
- 1/2 cup shredded cheddar cheese
- 1/4 cup diced red onion
- Two tablespoons chopped fresh cilantro
- 1 teaspoon garlic powder
- 1/2 teaspoon smoked paprika
- 1/4 teaspoon salt
- 1/4 teaspoon black pepper
- BBQ sauce for serving

Directions:

1. Preheat your grill to medium-high heat.
2. Slice each jalapeno pepper in half lengthwise. Remove the seeds and membrane using a spoon. Wear gloves or wash your hands thoroughly afterwards to avoid any irritation.
3. In a mixing bowl, combine the cream cheese, shredded cheddar cheese, diced red onion, chopped cilantro, garlic

powder, smoked paprika, salt, and black pepper. Mix well until all ingredients are evenly incorporated.

4. Spoon the cream cheese mixture into each jalapeno half, filling them generously.
5. Take a slice of bacon and wrap it around each stuffed jalapeno, securing it with toothpicks if needed. Repeat this step for all the jalapenos.
6. Place the bacon-wrapped jalapenos on the preheated grill. Cook for about 15-20 minutes, turning occasionally, until the bacon is crispy and the jalapenos are tender.
7. Once cooked, remove the jalapenos from the grill and allow them to cool for a few minutes. Carefully remove the toothpicks.
8. Serve the BBQ Bacon-Wrapped Stuffed Jalapenos with your favourite BBQ sauce for dipping. They can be served as an appetizer or as a delicious side dish.

Nutrition Facts (per serving):
- Calories: 195
- Fat: 16g
- Saturated Fat: 8g
- Cholesterol: 47mg
- Sodium: 345mg
- Carbohydrates: 4g
- Fibre: 1g
- Sugar: 2g
- Protein: 8g

Note: The nutrition facts may vary depending on the specific ingredients and quantities used.

GRILLED LEMON PEPPER CHICKEN

Prep Time: 10 minutes Cooking Time: 15 minutes Serving: 4 servings

Ingredients:

- Four boneless, skinless chicken breasts
- Two lemons
- Two tablespoons of olive oil
- One tablespoon of freshly ground black pepper
- One teaspoon salt
- One teaspoon of garlic powder
- One teaspoon paprika
- Fresh parsley for garnish (optional)

Directions:

1. Preheat your grill to medium-high heat.
2. In a small bowl, zest one lemon and squeeze the juice from both lemons.
3. In a separate bowl, combine the lemon zest, lemon juice, olive oil, black pepper, salt, garlic powder, and paprika. Mix well to create a marinade.
4. Place the chicken breasts in a shallow dish and pour the marinade over them. Make sure each breast is coated evenly. Allow the chicken to marinate for at least 10 minutes or up to 1 hour in the refrigerator.
5. Once the grill is hot, remove the chicken from the marinade and shake off any excess. Discard the remaining marinade.

6. Place the chicken breasts on the preheated grill. Cook for about 6-7 minutes on each side or until the internal temperature reaches 165°F (74°C) using a meat thermometer.
7. Remove the chicken from the grill and let it rest for a few minutes. This will help the juices distribute evenly throughout the meat.
8. Garnish with fresh parsley (optional) and serve hot.

Nutrition Facts (per serving):
- Calories: 250
- Total Fat: 10g
- Saturated Fat: 2g
- Cholesterol: 90mg
- Sodium: 600mg
- Carbohydrates: 3g
- Fibre: 1g
- Sugar: 0g
- Protein: 35g

Note: The nutrition facts provided are estimates and may vary depending on the ingredients used.

SHRIMP AND ANDOUILLE SAUSAGE JAMBALAYA

Prep Time: 20 minutes Cooking Time: 45 minutes Serving: 6 servings

Ingredients:
- 1 pound shrimp, peeled and deveined
- 8 ounces of andouille sausage, sliced

- One onion, diced
- One green bell pepper, diced
- Two celery stalks, diced
- Three cloves garlic, minced
- One can (14.5 ounces) of diced tomatoes
- 1 cup long-grain white rice
- 2 cups chicken broth
- One teaspoon paprika
- One teaspoon of dried thyme
- 1/2 teaspoon cayenne pepper (adjust according to your spice preference)
- Salt and black pepper to taste
- Two tablespoons of vegetable oil
- Fresh parsley, chopped (for garnish)

Directions:

1. Heat the vegetable oil over medium heat in a large skillet or Dutch oven.
2. Add the andouille sausage and cook until browned about 5 minutes. Remove the sausage from the skillet and set aside.
3. Add the onion, bell pepper, and celery in the same skillet. Sauté until the vegetables are softened, about 5 minutes.
4. Add the minced garlic and cook for an additional 1 minute.
5. Stir in the diced tomatoes (with their juice), rice, chicken broth, paprika, dried thyme, cayenne pepper, salt, and black pepper. Bring the mixture to a boil.

6. Reduce the heat to low, cover, and let it simmer for 20-25 minutes, or until the rice is cooked and the liquid is absorbed.
7. While the rice is cooking, season the shrimp with salt and black pepper.
8. Heat a small amount of oil over medium-high heat in a separate skillet. Cook the shrimp until pink and cooked through, about 2-3 minutes per side. Remove from the skillet and set aside.
9. Once the rice is cooked, add the cooked andouille sausage and shrimp to the skillet. Stir everything together gently to combine.
10. Cook for 2-3 minutes to heat the sausage and shrimp.
11. Remove from heat and garnish with chopped parsley.
12. Serve the Shrimp and Andouille Sausage Jambalaya hot, and enjoy!

Nutrition Facts (per serving):
- Calories: 370
- Total Fat: 15g
- Saturated Fat: 4g
- Cholesterol: 140mg
- Sodium: 900mg
- Total Carbohydrate: 36g
- Dietary Fiber: 3g
- Sugars: 5g
- Protein: 23g

Please note that the nutrition facts are approximate and may vary based on the ingredients used.

GRILLED MEDITERRANEAN VEGGIE SKEWERS

Prep Time: 20 minutes Cooking Time: 10 minutes Serving: 4

Ingredients:
- Two bell peppers (any colour), cut into chunks
- One zucchini, sliced into rounds
- One eggplant, cut into chunks
- One red onion, cut into chunks
- Eight cherry tomatoes
- Eight button mushrooms
- Two tablespoons of olive oil
- Two cloves garlic, minced
- One teaspoon of dried oregano
- One teaspoon of dried basil
- Salt and pepper, to taste
- Wooden skewers, soaked in water for 30 minutes

Directions:
1. Preheat your grill to medium-high heat.
2. In a large bowl, combine the olive oil, minced garlic, dried oregano, dried basil, salt, and pepper. Mix well.
3. Thread the vegetables onto the soaked wooden skewers, alternating between the different veggies. Leave some space between each piece to ensure even cooking.
4. Brush the vegetable skewers with the prepared olive oil and herb mixture, coating them evenly.

5. Place the skewers on the preheated grill and cook for about 10 minutes, turning occasionally, until the vegetables are tender and have grill marks.
6. Once cooked, remove the skewers from the grill and let them cool for a few minutes.
7. Serve the grilled Mediterranean veggie skewers hot as a side dish or as a main course with your favourite sauce or dip.

Nutrition Facts (per serving):

- Calories: 120
- Total Fat: 7g
- Saturated Fat: 1g
- Cholesterol: 0mg
- Sodium: 10mg
- Total Carbohydrate: 14g
- Dietary Fiber: 5g
- Sugars: 8g
- Protein: 3g

Note: Nutrition facts may vary depending on the specific ingredients used and any additional sauces or dips you may choose to serve with the skewers.

BBQ PULLED PORK NACHOS

Prep Time: 20 minutes Cooking Time: 4 hours Serving: 6-8 servings

Ingredients:

- 2 pounds of boneless pork shoulder
- One tablespoon of vegetable oil

- 1 cup BBQ sauce
- 1 cup shredded cheddar cheese
- 1/2 cup diced red onion
- 1/4 cup chopped fresh cilantro
- One jalapeno pepper, thinly sliced (optional)
- One bag of tortilla chips
- Salt and pepper to taste

Directions:
1. Preheat your oven to 325°F (163°C).
2. Season the pork shoulder with salt and pepper on all sides.
3. Heat the vegetable oil in a large oven-safe pot or Dutch oven over medium-high heat. Add the pork shoulder and sear it on all sides until browned, about 5 minutes per side.
4. Once the pork is browned, remove it from the pot and set it aside. Pour off any excess fat from the pot.
5. Return the pot to the stove and reduce the heat to medium. Add the BBQ sauce and stir it to scrape up any browned bits from the bottom of the pot.
6. Place the pork shoulder back into the pot, cover it with a lid, and transfer it to the preheated oven.
7. Allow the pork to cook in the oven for about 4 hours or until it is tender and easily shreds apart with a fork.
8. Once the pork is cooked, remove it from the oven and transfer it to a cutting board. Use two forks to shred the meat into bite-sized pieces.
9. Preheat your broiler.
10. Arrange the tortilla chips in a single layer on a baking sheet or oven-safe platter.

11. Spread the shredded pork evenly over the tortilla chips.

12. Sprinkle the shredded cheddar cheese, diced red onion, and jalapeno slices (if desired) over the pork.

13. Place the nachos under the broiler for 2-3 minutes or until the cheese is melted and bubbly.

14. Remove the nachos from the broiler and garnish with chopped cilantro.

15. Serve the BBQ Pulled Pork Nachos immediately while they are still hot, and enjoy!

Nutrition Facts (per serving): Calories: 450 Total Fat: 24g Saturated Fat: 9g Cholesterol: 95mg Sodium: 730mg Total Carbohydrate: 32g Dietary Fiber: 2g Sugars: 15g Protein: 26g

Note: Nutrition facts are approximate and may vary depending on the ingredients used.

Was this response better or worse?

BetterWorseSame

GRILLED TERIYAKI PINEAPPLE CHICKEN

Prep Time: 15 minutes Cooking Time: 20 minutes Serving: 4 servings

Ingredients:

- Four boneless, skinless chicken breasts
- 1 cup teriyaki sauce
- 1/4 cup pineapple juice
- Two tablespoons of soy sauce
- Two tablespoons honey
- Two cloves garlic, minced

- One teaspoon of ginger, grated
- 1/2 teaspoon black pepper
- 1/2 teaspoon red pepper flakes (optional)
- Four pineapple rings
- Two green onions, chopped (for garnish)

Directions:

1. In a bowl, combine teriyaki sauce, pineapple juice, soy sauce, honey, minced garlic, grated ginger, black pepper, and red pepper flakes (if desired). Mix well to make the marinade.
2. Place the chicken breasts in a ziplock bag or a shallow dish. Pour the marinade over the chicken, making sure it is evenly coated. Seal the bag or cover the dish with plastic wrap. Let it marinate in the refrigerator for at least 1 hour or overnight for best results.
3. Preheat the grill to medium-high heat.
4. Remove the chicken from the marinade, allowing any excess marinade to drip off. Reserve the marinade for later use.
5. Place the chicken breasts on the preheated grill and cook for about 8-10 minutes per side, or until the chicken is fully cooked through and the internal temperature reaches 165°F (74°C).
6. While the chicken is grilling, brush the pineapple rings with the reserved marinade and place them on the grill. Cook for 2-3 minutes per side or until the pineapple is lightly charred and caramelized.
7. Once the chicken is cooked, remove it from the grill and let it rest for a few minutes. Then, slice it into thin strips.

8. Serve the grilled teriyaki pineapple chicken with the grilled pineapple rings on the side. Garnish with chopped green onions.

9. Enjoy your delicious Grilled Teriyaki Pineapple Chicken!

Nutrition Facts (per serving):

- Calories: 320
- Total Fat: 4g
- Saturated Fat: 1g
- Cholesterol: 96mg
- Sodium: 1050mg
- Total Carbohydrate: 30g
- Dietary Fiber: 1g
- Sugars: 25g
- Protein: 40g

Note: The nutrition facts may vary depending on the specific brands of ingredients used and any modifications made to the recipe.

BACON-WRAPPED STUFFED MUSHROOMS

Prep Time: 20 minutes Cooking Time: 25 minutes Serving: 4-6 servings

Ingredients:

- 24 button mushrooms
- 12 slices of bacon
- 1/2 cup cream cheese, softened
- 1/4 cup grated Parmesan cheese

- Two cloves garlic, minced
- One tablespoon of chopped fresh parsley
- 1/2 teaspoon dried thyme
- Salt and pepper to taste

Directions:

1. Preheat your oven to 375°F (190°C). Line a baking sheet with parchment paper or aluminium foil for easy cleanup.
2. Clean the mushrooms and remove the stems. Set aside.
3. In a bowl, combine the softened cream cheese, grated Parmesan cheese, minced garlic, chopped parsley, dried thyme, salt, and pepper. Mix well until all the ingredients are evenly incorporated.
4. Take a mushroom cap and stuff it with the cream cheese mixture. Repeat with the remaining mushrooms and filling.
5. Take a slice of bacon and cut it in half crosswise. Wrap each stuffed mushroom with a half slice of bacon, securing it with a toothpick if necessary. Repeat until all the mushrooms are wrapped.
6. Arrange the bacon-wrapped mushrooms on the prepared baking sheet, spacing them apart to allow for even cooking.
7. Place the baking sheet in the preheated oven and bake for 20-25 minutes, or until the bacon is crispy and the mushrooms are tender.
8. Once cooked, remove the toothpicks from the mushrooms and transfer them to a serving platter.
9. Serve the bacon-wrapped stuffed mushrooms hot as an appetizer or snack.

Nutrition Facts (per serving):

- Calories: 180
- Total Fat: 13g
- Saturated Fat: 6g
- Cholesterol: 37mg
- Sodium: 375mg
- Total Carbohydrate: 4g
- Dietary Fiber: 1g
- Sugars: 2g
- Protein: 10g

Note: The nutrition facts provided are approximate and may vary depending on the specific ingredients used.

GRILLED LEMON GARLIC SHRIMP SCAMPI PASTA

Prep Time: 15 minutes Cooking Time: 15 minutes Serving: 4 servings

Ingredients:
- 1 pound (450g) shrimp, peeled and deveined
- 8 ounces (225g) linguine or spaghetti
- Four tablespoons olive oil divided
- Four cloves garlic, minced
- 1/2 teaspoon red pepper flakes (optional)
- One lemon, zested and juiced
- Salt and black pepper to taste
- 1/4 cup fresh parsley, chopped
- Grated Parmesan cheese for garnish

Directions:

1. Preheat your grill to medium-high heat.
2. Cook the linguine or spaghetti according to the package instructions until al dente. Drain and set aside.
3. In a large bowl, combine two tablespoons of olive oil, minced garlic, red pepper flakes (if using), lemon zest, lemon juice, salt, and black pepper. Add the shrimp to the bowl and toss to coat them evenly.
4. Thread the shrimp onto skewers and grill for 2-3 minutes per side or until they turn pink and are cooked through. Remove the shrimp from the skewers and set them aside.
5. Heat the remaining two tablespoons of olive oil over medium heat in a large skillet. Add the cooked linguine or spaghetti to the skillet and toss to coat it with the olive oil.
6. Add the grilled shrimp to the skillet and toss gently to combine. Cook for an additional 1-2 minutes to heat through.
7. Remove the skillet from the heat and sprinkle the chopped parsley over the pasta. Toss once more to distribute the parsley evenly.
8. Serve the grilled lemon garlic shrimp scampi pasta hot, garnished with grated Parmesan cheese.

Nutrition Facts (per serving):
- Calories: 380
- Total Fat: 14g
- Saturated Fat: 2g
- Cholesterol: 172mg
- Sodium: 250mg
- Carbohydrates: 35g

- Fibre: 2g
- Sugar: 2g
- Protein: 26g

Note: Nutrition facts are approximate and may vary depending on the ingredients used.

BUFFALO CHICKEN SLIDERS

Prep Time: 15 minutes Cooking Time: 20 minutes Servings: 4

Ingredients:
- 1 pound boneless, skinless chicken breasts
- 1/2 cup buffalo sauce
- 1/4 cup melted butter
- 1/2 teaspoon garlic powder
- Salt and pepper to taste
- Eight slider buns
- Blue cheese dressing (optional)
- Lettuce and tomato slices (optional)

Directions:
1. Preheat your grill or stovetop grill pan over medium-high heat.
2. Season the chicken breasts with garlic powder, salt, and pepper.
3. In a small bowl, mix the buffalo sauce and melted butter.
4. Brush the buffalo sauce mixture onto the chicken breasts, ensuring they are well coated.

5. Place the chicken breasts on the preheated grill and cook for about 6-8 minutes per side or until the internal temperature reaches 165°F (74°C).
6. While the chicken is cooking, lightly toast the slider buns on the grill or in a toaster.
7. Once the chicken is cooked, remove it from the grill and let it rest for a few minutes.
8. Slice the chicken breasts into thin strips or shred them using two forks.
9. Place the chicken on the slider buns and drizzle with additional buffalo sauce if desired.
10. Optional: Add a dollop of blue cheese dressing on top of the chicken and top with lettuce and tomato slices.
11. Serve the Buffalo Chicken Sliders warm, and enjoy!

Nutrition Facts (per serving):
- Calories: 350
- Total Fat: 12g
- Saturated Fat: 6g
- Cholesterol: 100mg
- Sodium: 1000mg
- Carbohydrates: 26g
- Fibre: 2g
- Sugars: 2g
- Protein: 32g

Note: The nutrition facts are approximate and may vary depending on the ingredients used.

GRILLED BRUSCHETTA CHICKEN

Prep Time: 15 minutes Cooking Time: 20 minutes Serving: 4 servings

Ingredients:

- Four boneless, skinless chicken breasts
- Two tablespoons of olive oil
- Salt and black pepper to taste
- Four slices of Italian bread or baguette
- Two cloves of garlic peeled
- Four ripe tomatoes, diced
- ½ cup fresh basil leaves, chopped
- ½ cup shredded mozzarella cheese
- Balsamic glaze for drizzling (optional)

Directions:

1. Preheat your grill to medium-high heat.
2. Brush the chicken breasts with olive oil and season them with salt and black pepper on both sides.
3. Place the chicken breasts on the grill and cook for about 6-8 minutes per side or until they are cooked through and have nice grill marks. Remove from the grill and set aside.
4. While the chicken is cooking, preheat your oven's broiler.
5. Place the slices of bread on a baking sheet and broil them for about 2-3 minutes per side or until they are toasted and golden brown. Remove from the oven and rub one side of each slice with the garlic cloves.
6. In a bowl, combine the diced tomatoes and chopped basil. Season with salt and black pepper to taste.

7. Spoon the tomato and basil mixture over the garlic-rubbed side of each toasted bread slice.
8. Slice the grilled chicken breasts and place the slices on top of the tomato and basil mixture.
9. Sprinkle the shredded mozzarella cheese over the chicken.
10. Place the assembled bruschetta onto the baking sheet and broil for 2-3 minutes or until the cheese is melted and bubbly.
11. Remove from the oven and let it cool for a minute.
12. Serve the Grilled Bruschetta Chicken immediately, drizzled with balsamic glaze if desired.

Nutrition Facts (per serving):
- Calories: 320
- Total Fat: 11g
- Saturated Fat: 3g
- Cholesterol: 85mg
- Sodium: 450mg
- Carbohydrates: 15g
- Fibre: 2g
- Sugars: 4g
- Protein: 38g

Note: Nutrition facts may vary depending on the specific ingredients and brands used.

BBQ PULLED PORK STUFFED SWEET POTATOES

Prep Time: 20 minutes Cooking Time: 4 hours Serving: 4 servings

Ingredients:

- Four medium-sized sweet potatoes
- 1.5 pounds (680 grams) of boneless pork shoulder
- 1 cup barbecue sauce
- 1/2 cup chicken broth
- One tablespoon of olive oil
- One small onion, finely chopped
- Two cloves garlic, minced
- One teaspoon smoked paprika
- 1/2 teaspoon chilli powder
- Salt and pepper to taste
- Optional toppings: shredded cheese, sliced green onions, sour cream

Directions:

1. Preheat your oven to 400°F (200°C).
2. Wash the sweet potatoes thoroughly and prick them all over with a fork. Place them on a baking sheet and bake for 45-60 minutes or until tender. Remove from the oven and set aside.
3. While the sweet potatoes are baking, prepare the pulled pork. Season the pork shoulder with salt, pepper, smoked paprika, and chilli powder.
4. Heat olive oil in a large skillet or Dutch oven over medium-high heat. Add the seasoned pork shoulder and sear it on all sides until browned, about 5 minutes per side.
5. Remove the pork from the skillet and set it aside. In the same skillet, add chopped onion and minced garlic. Sauté until the onion becomes translucent and fragrant.

6. Return the seared pork to the skillet and add barbecue sauce and chicken broth. Stir well to combine.
7. Reduce the heat to low, cover the skillet, and simmer for 3-4 hours or until the pork becomes tender and easy to shred.
8. Once the pork is cooked, shred it into smaller pieces using two forks. Mix it with the sauce in the skillet to coat the meat evenly.
9. To assemble, cut a slit lengthwise in each baked sweet potato. Gently push the ends toward the centre to open up a pocket.
10. Spoon a generous amount of BBQ-pulled pork into each sweet potato pocket.
11. If desired, top the stuffed sweet potatoes with shredded cheese and return them to the oven for a few minutes until the cheese melts.
12. Serve the BBQ-pulled pork stuffed sweet potatoes hot, garnished with sliced green onions and a dollop of sour cream.

Nutrition Facts (per serving):
- Calories: 420
- Total Fat: 12g
- Saturated Fat: 3g
- Cholesterol: 75mg
- Sodium: 680mg
- Carbohydrate: 53g
- Fibre: 6g
- Sugar: 24g
- Protein: 27g

Note: The nutrition facts may vary based on the specific brands of ingredients used and any optional toppings added.

GRILLED TERIYAKI BEEF STIR-FRY

Prep Time: 15 minutes Cooking Time: 15 minutes Serving: 4 servings

Ingredients:
- 1 pound beef sirloin, thinly sliced
- 1/4 cup teriyaki sauce
- Two tablespoons soy sauce
- Two tablespoons honey
- Two cloves garlic, minced
- One teaspoon grated ginger
- One tablespoon vegetable oil
- One red bell pepper, sliced
- One yellow bell pepper, sliced
- One small onion, sliced
- 1 cup broccoli florets
- 1 cup snap peas
- Salt and pepper, to taste
- Cooked rice for serving
- Sesame seeds, for garnish (optional)
- Green onions, sliced, for garnish (optional)

Directions:

1. Combine the teriyaki sauce, soy sauce, honey, minced garlic, and grated ginger in a bowl. Add the sliced beef to the bowl and marinate for at least 10 minutes.
2. Heat a grill or grill pan over medium-high heat. Remove the beef from the marinade, allowing any excess marinade to drip off. Grill the beef for 2-3 minutes per side or until it reaches your desired level of doneness. Remove the beef from the grill and let it rest for a few minutes. Slice the grilled beef into thin strips.
3. Heat the vegetable oil over medium heat in a large skillet or wok. Add the sliced bell peppers, onion, broccoli, and snap peas to the skillet. Stir-fry the vegetables for 4-5 minutes or until they are tender-crisp.
4. Add the sliced grilled beef to the skillet with the vegetables. Pour any remaining marinade over the beef and vegetables. Stir-fry everything together for an additional 2-3 minutes or until the beef is heated through and the flavours are well combined. Season with salt and pepper to taste.
5. Serve the Grilled Teriyaki Beef Stir-Fry over cooked rice. Garnish with sesame seeds and sliced green onions, if desired.

Nutrition Facts (per serving):
- Calories: 320
- Fat: 12g
- Saturated Fat: 3.5g
- Cholesterol: 75mg
- Sodium: 980mg
- Carbohydrates: 25g
- Fibre: 4g

- Sugar: 15g
- Protein: 27g

Note: The nutrition facts are approximate and may vary based on the specific ingredients used.

GRILLED CAJUN SHRIMP PO'BOY SANDWICH

Prep Time: 20 minutes Cooking Time: 10 minutes Servings: 4

Ingredients:

- 1 pound large shrimp, peeled and deveined
- Two tablespoons of Cajun seasoning
- Two tablespoons of olive oil
- 4 French bread rolls
- 1/4 cup mayonnaise
- Two tablespoons of Creole mustard
- One tablespoon of hot sauce (optional)
- 1 cup shredded lettuce
- One tomato, sliced
- 1/2 cup sliced pickles
- Salt and pepper to taste

Directions:

1. Preheat your grill or grill pan to medium-high heat.
2. In a mixing bowl, combine the shrimp, Cajun seasoning, olive oil, salt, and pepper. Toss well to coat the shrimp evenly.
3. Grill the shrimp for about 2-3 minutes per side until they turn pink and opaque. Remove from heat and set aside.
4. Slice the French bread rolls lengthwise, leaving one side intact to form a hinge.
5. Mix the mayonnaise, Creole mustard, and hot sauce (if using).
6. Spread the mayonnaise mixture on both sides of the bread rolls.

7. Layer the grilled shrimp on the bottom half of the bread rolls.
8. Top the shrimp with shredded lettuce, tomato slices, and sliced pickles.
9. Close the sandwich and press it down gently.
10. If desired, you can wrap the sandwich in aluminium foil and warm it on the grill for a few minutes to melt the flavours together.
11. Slice the sandwich into individual servings and serve immediately.

Nutrition Facts (per serving):
- Calories: 380
- Fat: 15g
- Saturated Fat: 2g
- Cholesterol: 220mg
- Sodium: 1000mg
- Carbohydrates: 37g
- Fibre: 3g
- Sugar: 5g
- Protein: 25g

Enjoy your delicious Grilled Cajun Shrimp Po' Boy Sandwich!

GRILLED HONEY MUSTARD CHICKEN

Prep Time: 10 minutes Cooking Time: 20 minutes Serving: 4 servings

Ingredients:
- 4 boneless, skinless chicken breasts

- 1/4 cup Dijon mustard
- 1/4 cup honey
- Two tablespoons of olive oil
- Two tablespoons of lemon juice
- Two cloves garlic, minced
- One teaspoon paprika
- 1/2 teaspoon salt
- 1/4 teaspoon black pepper
- Fresh parsley, chopped (for garnish)

Directions:

1. Preheat your grill to medium-high heat.
2. In a small bowl, whisk together the Dijon mustard, honey, olive oil, lemon juice, minced garlic, paprika, salt, and black pepper until well combined.
3. Place the chicken breasts in a shallow dish or a resealable plastic bag. Pour the honey mustard marinade over the chicken, coating each piece thoroughly. Allow the chicken to marinate for at least 30 minutes, or refrigerate for up to 4 hours for maximum flavour.
4. Remove the chicken from the marinade and discard any excess marinade.
5. Place the chicken breasts on the preheated grill. Cook for about 8-10 minutes per side or until the chicken is cooked through and reaches an internal temperature of 165°F (75°C).
6. Once cooked, remove the chicken from the grill and let it rest for a few minutes.

7. Garnish with fresh chopped parsley and serve hot with your favourite side dishes or a fresh salad.

Nutrition Facts (per serving):

- Calories: 280
- Total Fat: 9g
- Saturated Fat: 1.5g
- Cholesterol: 80mg
- Sodium: 480mg
- Carbohydrates: 16g
- Fibre: 0.5g
- Sugar: 15g
- Protein: 31g

Note: The nutrition facts are approximate and may vary depending on the specific ingredients used and the portion sizes.

Enjoy your delicious Grilled Honey Mustard Chicken!

GRILLED STUFFED BELL PEPPERS

Prep Time: 20 minutes Cooking Time: 30 minutes Serving: 4

Ingredients:

- Four large bell peppers (any colour)
- 1 cup cooked quinoa
- 1 cup cooked black beans
- 1 cup corn kernels (fresh or frozen)
- One small onion, finely chopped
- Two cloves garlic, minced
- One jalapeno pepper, seeded and minced (optional)

- 1 cup shredded cheese (cheddar, mozzarella, or a blend)
- One teaspoon cumin
- One teaspoon chilli powder
- Salt and pepper to taste
- Olive oil

Directions:

1. Preheat your grill to medium heat.
2. Cut the tops off the bell peppers and remove the seeds and membranes from the inside. Rinse the peppers thoroughly.
3. In a large mixing bowl, combine the cooked quinoa, black beans, corn, onion, garlic, jalapeno pepper (if using), cumin, chilli powder, salt, and pepper. Mix well to combine all the ingredients.
4. Spoon the quinoa and bean mixture into each bell pepper, filling them to the top. Press down gently to pack the mixture inside.
5. Sprinkle the shredded cheese over the top of each stuffed pepper.
6. Lightly brush the outside of each pepper with olive oil to prevent sticking to the grill.
7. Place the stuffed bell peppers on the preheated grill. Close the lid and cook for about 25-30 minutes or until the peppers are tender and the cheese is melted and lightly browned.
8. Carefully remove the stuffed bell peppers from the grill using tongs or a spatula. Allow them to cool for a few minutes before serving.
9. Serve the grilled stuffed bell peppers as a main dish or a side dish. They pair well with a fresh salad or rice.

Nutrition Facts (per serving):
- Calories: 300
- Fat: 10g
- Carbohydrates: 40g
- Fibre: 10g
- Protein: 15g
- Vitamin C: 150% DV
- Calcium: 25% DV
- Iron: 20% DV

Note: The nutrition facts are approximate and may vary depending on the ingredients used.

BBQ CHICKEN FLATBREAD PIZZA

Prep Time: 15 minutes Cooking Time: 15 minutes Servings: 4

Ingredients:
- Two large flatbreads or naan loaves of bread
- 1 cup cooked chicken breast, shredded or diced
- 1/2 cup barbecue sauce
- 1 cup shredded mozzarella cheese
- 1/4 red onion, thinly sliced
- 1/4 cup fresh cilantro leaves, chopped
- Olive oil for brushing

Directions:
1. Preheat the oven to 425°F (220°C).
2. Place the flatbreads on a baking sheet. Brush the tops with a little olive oil.

3. In a small bowl, mix the shredded chicken with barbecue sauce until well coated.
4. Spread half of the barbecue chicken mixture evenly over each flatbread.
5. Sprinkle the shredded mozzarella cheese over the chicken.
6. Arrange the thinly sliced red onions on top of the cheese.
7. Place the baking sheet in the preheated oven and bake for about 12-15 minutes, or until the cheese is melted and bubbly and the flatbread edges are crispy.
8. Remove from the oven and let the flatbreads cool slightly.
9. Sprinkle the chopped cilantro over the top of the pizzas.
10. Slice the flatbreads into wedges and serve hot.

Nutrition Facts (per serving):
- Calories: 325
- Fat: 11g
- Saturated Fat: 4g
- Cholesterol: 46mg
- Sodium: 763mg
- Carbohydrates: 35g
- Fibre: 2g
- Sugar: 16g
- Protein: 20g

Note: The nutrition facts are approximate and may vary depending on the specific ingredients and brands used.

GRILLED PINEAPPLE TERIYAKI BURGERS

Prep Time: 15 minutes Cooking Time: 20 minutes Serving: 4 burgers

Ingredients:

- 1 pound ground beef
- Four pineapple slices
- Four burger buns
- Four slices of cheddar cheese
- 1/4 cup teriyaki sauce
- 1/4 cup mayonnaise
- Four lettuce leaves
- One tomato, sliced
- Salt and pepper to taste

Directions:

1. Preheat the grill to medium-high heat.
2. In a bowl, season the ground beef with salt and pepper. Mix well to combine.
3. Divide the ground beef mixture into four equal portions and shape them into burger patties.
4. Place the pineapple slices on the grill and cook for 2-3 minutes on each side until grill marks appear. Remove from the grill and set aside.
5. Place the burger patties on the preheated grill and cook for about 4-5 minutes on each side or until they reach your desired level of doneness.
6. During the last few minutes of cooking, brush each burger patty with teriyaki sauce, flipping once to ensure both sides are coated.

7. While the burgers are cooking, lightly toast the burger buns on the grill.
8. Assemble the burgers by spreading mayonnaise on the bottom half of each bun. Top with a lettuce leaf, a burger patty, a slice of cheddar cheese, a grilled pineapple slice, and a few slices of tomato.
9. Serve the Grilled Pineapple Teriyaki Burgers with your favourite side dish, and enjoy!

Nutrition Facts (per serving):
- Calories: 480
- Fat: 26g
- Saturated Fat: 9g
- Cholesterol: 80mg
- Sodium: 900mg
- Carbohydrates: 36g
- Fibre: 3g
- Sugar: 14g
- Protein: 26g
- Vitamin D: 2mcg
- Calcium: 220mg
- Iron: 4mg
- Potassium: 460mg

Note: The nutrition facts are approximate and may vary depending on the specific ingredients and brands used.

BACON-WRAPPED BBQ CHICKEN SKEWERS

Prep Time: 15 minutes Cooking Time: 25 minutes Serving: 4 servings

Ingredients:

- Four boneless, skinless chicken breasts
- Eight slices of bacon
- 1 cup of your favourite BBQ sauce
- One teaspoon of garlic powder
- One teaspoon paprika
- Salt and pepper, to taste
- Wooden skewers, soaked in water for 30 minutes

Directions:

1. Preheat your grill to medium-high heat.
2. Cut each chicken breast into bite-sized chunks.
3. Mix the garlic powder, paprika, salt, and pepper in a small bowl.
4. Season the chicken chunks with the spice mixture, ensuring they are evenly coated.
5. Take a slice of bacon and wrap it around a piece of chicken. Thread the bacon-wrapped chicken onto a soaked wooden skewer. Repeat this process until all the chicken pieces are wrapped and skewered.
6. Place the bacon-wrapped chicken skewers on the preheated grill. Cook for about 8-10 minutes per side or until the bacon is crispy and the chicken is cooked through.
7. Brush the BBQ sauce onto the skewers during the last few minutes of cooking, turning them once to ensure even coverage. Reserve some BBQ sauce for dipping.

8. Once the chicken is fully cooked and the bacon is crispy, remove the skewers from the grill.
9. Serve the Bacon-Wrapped BBQ Chicken Skewers hot, with the reserved BBQ sauce for dipping.

Nutrition Facts (per serving):

- Calories: 320
- Fat: 12g
- Saturated Fat: 4g
- Cholesterol: 100mg
- Sodium: 980mg
- Carbohydrates: 18g
- Fibre: 0g
- Sugar: 14g
- Protein: 33g

Note: The nutrition facts provided are estimates and may vary depending on the specific ingredients used and the serving size.

GRILLED RATATOUILLE

Prep Time: 15 minutes Cooking Time: 25 minutes Serving: 4

Ingredients:

- One medium eggplant, sliced into 1/2-inch rounds
- Two small zucchini, sliced into 1/2-inch rounds
- One red bell pepper, seeded and cut into chunks
- One yellow bell pepper, seeded and cut into chunks
- One red onion, cut into chunks
- Two tablespoons of olive oil

- Two cloves garlic, minced
- One teaspoon of dried thyme
- One teaspoon of dried oregano
- Salt and pepper to taste
- Fresh basil leaves for garnish

Directions:

1. Preheat your grill to medium-high heat.
2. In a large bowl, combine the eggplant, zucchini, bell peppers, and onion. Drizzle with olive oil and toss to coat the vegetables evenly.
3. Mix the minced garlic, dried thyme, oregano, salt, and pepper in a small bowl. Sprinkle the herb mixture over the vegetables and toss again to ensure they are well coated.
4. Place the seasoned vegetables directly on the grill grates. Grill for 10-12 minutes, flipping once halfway through or until the vegetables are tender and slightly charred.
5. Remove the grilled vegetables from the grill and transfer them to a serving platter. Allow them to cool slightly.
6. Garnish with fresh basil leaves before serving. You can also drizzle some extra olive oil on top if desired.

Nutrition Facts (per serving):

- Calories: 120
- Fat: 7g
- Carbohydrates: 14g
- Fibre: 5g
- Protein: 3g

Note: The nutrition facts are approximate and may vary based on the specific ingredients and quantities used.

CHIPOTLE LIME GRILLED SHRIMP

Prep Time: 15 minutes Cooking Time: 5 minutes Serving: 4 servings

Ingredients:

- 1 pound large shrimp, peeled and deveined
- Two tablespoons of olive oil
- Two cloves garlic, minced
- One chipotle pepper in adobo sauce, minced
- One tablespoon of lime zest
- Two tablespoons of lime juice
- One teaspoon honey
- 1/2 teaspoon salt
- Freshly ground black pepper, to taste
- Lime wedges for serving
- Fresh cilantro for garnish

Directions:

1. Preheat the grill to medium-high heat.
2. In a bowl, combine the olive oil, minced garlic, chipotle pepper, lime zest, lime juice, honey, salt, and black pepper. Stir well to combine.
3. Add the shrimp to the bowl and toss to coat them evenly with the marinade. Let the shrimp marinate for about 10 minutes.
4. Thread the shrimp onto skewers, piercing them through the tail, and the head end to keep them in place.

5. Place the shrimp skewers on the preheated grill and cook for about 2-3 minutes per side or until they turn pink and opaque.
6. Remove the shrimp from the grill and transfer them to a serving platter.
7. Garnish with fresh cilantro and serve with lime wedges on the side for squeezing over the shrimp.
8. Enjoy your delicious chipotle lime-grilled shrimp!

Nutrition Facts (per serving):
- Calories: 180
- Fat: 9g
- Saturated Fat: 1.5g
- Cholesterol: 200mg
- Sodium: 380mg
- Carbohydrates: 3g
- Fibre: 0.5g
- Sugar: 1g
- Protein: 21g
- Vitamin D: 10% DV
- Calcium: 10% DV
- Iron: 15% DV
- Potassium: 250mg

GRILLED SAUSAGE AND PEPPERS

Prep Time: 15 minutes Cooking Time: 20 minutes Serving: 4 servings

Ingredients:

- 4 Italian sausages (mild or spicy, your choice)
- Two bell peppers (any colour), seeded and sliced
- One large onion, sliced
- Two tablespoons of olive oil
- One teaspoon of dried oregano
- One teaspoon of garlic powder
- Salt and pepper to taste
- 4 hoagie rolls (optional)

Directions:

1. Preheat your grill to medium-high heat.
2. In a large bowl, combine the sliced bell peppers, onion, olive oil, dried oregano, garlic powder, salt, and pepper. Toss to coat the vegetables evenly.
3. Grill the sausages on the preheated grill for about 15-20 minutes, turning occasionally, until they are browned and cooked through. Remove from the grill and set aside.
4. While the sausages are grilling, place the seasoned peppers and onions on a grill pan or aluminium foil. Cook them on the grill, stirring occasionally, until they are tender and slightly charred, about 10-15 minutes.
5. Once the sausages and peppers are cooked, you can serve them separately or combine them. If desired, lightly toast the hoagie rolls on the grill.
6. To serve, place a sausage in each hoagie roll (or on a plate if not using rolls) and top with a generous portion of grilled peppers and onions.

Nutrition Facts (per serving):

- Calories: 350

- Total Fat: 25g
- Saturated Fat: 8g
- Cholesterol: 40mg
- Sodium: 750mg
- Total Carbohydrate: 23g
- Dietary Fiber: 3g
- Sugars: 5g
- Protein: 12g

Enjoy your delicious Grilled Sausage and Peppers!

BBQ PORK SLIDERS

Prep Time: 15 minutes Cooking Time: 4 hours Servings: 6
Ingredients:
- 2 pounds pork shoulder, boneless
- 1 cup BBQ sauce
- 1/4 cup brown sugar
- 1/4 cup apple cider vinegar
- One tablespoon of Worcestershire sauce
- One teaspoon of garlic powder
- One teaspoon of onion powder
- One teaspoon of smoked paprika
- 1/2 teaspoon salt
- 1/2 teaspoon black pepper
- 12 slider buns
- Coleslaw (optional for serving)

Directions:

1. In a slow cooker, combine BBQ sauce, brown sugar, apple cider vinegar, Worcestershire sauce, garlic powder, onion powder, smoked paprika, salt, and black pepper. Stir well to combine.
2. Add the pork shoulder to the slow cooker and turn it around to coat it evenly with the sauce mixture.
3. Cover the slow cooker and cook on low heat for 8 hours or on high heat for 4 hours or until the pork is tender and easily shreds with a fork.
4. Once the pork is cooked, remove it from the slow cooker and transfer it to a cutting board. Shred the pork using two forks.
5. Return the shredded pork to the slow cooker and mix it with the remaining sauce.
6. Heat the pork and sauce mixture on high heat for an additional 10-15 minutes, occasionally stirring, to allow the flavours to meld together.
7. Place a generous amount of BBQ pork onto each slider bun to assemble the sliders. If desired, top with coleslaw for added freshness and crunch.
8. Serve the BBQ pork sliders warm, and enjoy!

Nutrition Facts (per serving):

- Calories: 450
- Total Fat: 14g
- Saturated Fat: 5g
- Cholesterol: 85mg
- Sodium: 900mg
- Total Carbohydrate: 50g
- Dietary Fiber: 2g

- Sugars: 23g
- Protein: 30g

Note: The nutrition facts are approximate and may vary depending on the specific ingredients used and the serving size.

GRILLED TERIYAKI TOFU

Prep Time: 15 minutes Cooking Time: 15 minutes Serving: 4 servings

Ingredients:

- One block of firm tofu
- 1/4 cup soy sauce
- Two tablespoons of honey or maple syrup
- Two tablespoons of rice vinegar
- One tablespoon of sesame oil
- Two cloves of garlic, minced
- One teaspoon of grated ginger
- One tablespoon cornstarch
- Two tablespoons water
- Sesame seeds, for garnish
- Sliced green onions for garnish

Directions:

1. Start by pressing the tofu to remove excess water. Place the block of tofu on a plate lined with paper towels or a clean kitchen towel. Put another layer of paper towels or a kitchen towel on top of the tofu, and then place something heavy on top, like a cast iron skillet or a few heavy books. Let it sit for about 10 minutes to drain.

2. While the tofu is being pressed, prepare the teriyaki sauce. In a small bowl, whisk together the soy sauce, honey or maple syrup, rice vinegar, sesame oil, minced garlic, and grated ginger.
3. Once the tofu is drained, slice it into rectangular pieces about 1/2 inch thick.
4. Preheat your grill or grill pan over medium heat.
5. Brush the grill grates with a little oil to prevent sticking. Place the tofu slices on the grill and cook for about 5-7 minutes on each side until they develop grill marks and become firm.
6. While the tofu is grilling, pour the teriyaki sauce into a small saucepan and heat it over medium heat.
7. In a separate small bowl, whisk together the cornstarch and water to make a slurry. Add the slurry to the teriyaki sauce, stirring constantly until the sauce thickens. Remove from heat.
8. Once the tofu is cooked, remove it from the grill and brush both sides with the teriyaki sauce.
9. Garnish the grilled teriyaki tofu with sesame seeds and sliced green onions.
10. Serve the tofu hot with steamed rice or your favourite side dishes.

Nutrition Facts (per serving):
- Calories: 180
- Total Fat: 7g
- Saturated Fat: 1g
- Cholesterol: 0mg
- Sodium: 620mg

- Total Carbohydrate: 18g
- Dietary Fiber: 1g
- Sugars: 10g
- Protein: 12g

Note: Nutrition facts may vary depending on the brand and type of ingredients used.

PORTOBELLO MUSHROOM AND GOAT CHEESE BURGER

Prep Time: 15 minutes Cooking Time: 15 minutes Serving: 4 burgers

Ingredients:

- Four large portobello mushroom caps
- Four burger buns
- 4 ounces goat cheese, crumbled
- One red onion, thinly sliced
- 1 cup baby spinach leaves
- Two tablespoons balsamic vinegar
- Two tablespoons olive oil
- Salt and pepper to taste

Directions:

1. Preheat your grill or stovetop grill pan to medium-high heat.
2. Whisk together the balsamic vinegar, olive oil, salt, and pepper in a small bowl.
3. Brush the portobello mushroom caps on both sides with the balsamic mixture.

4. Place the mushrooms on the grill or grill pan and cook for about 4-5 minutes per side until tender and grill marks appear.
5. While the mushrooms are grilling, lightly toast the burger buns on the grill or in a toaster.
6. Remove the mushrooms from the grill and let them cool slightly. Then, thinly slice them.
7. To assemble the burgers, spread the crumbled goat cheese on the bottom half of each burger bun.
8. Top with a few slices of grilled portobello mushrooms, followed by red onion slices and baby spinach leaves.
9. Place the top half of the burger bun on each assembled burger.
10. Serve the Portobello Mushroom and Goat Cheese Burgers immediately, and enjoy!

Nutrition Facts (per serving): Calories: 280 Total Fat: 13g

- Saturated Fat: 5g
- Trans Fat: 0g Cholesterol: 10mg Sodium: 420mg Total Carbohydrate: 31g
- Dietary Fiber: 4g
- Sugars: 6g Protein: 11g Vitamin D: 0mcg Calcium: 70mg Iron: 3mg Potassium: 710mg

Note: The nutrition facts provided are estimates and may vary based on the specific ingredients used.

GRILLED MEDITERRANEAN CHICKEN SKEWERS

Prep Time: 20 minutes Cooking Time: 15 minutes Serving: 4

Ingredients:

- 1.5 pounds boneless, skinless chicken breasts cut into 1-inch cubes
- 1/4 cup olive oil
- Two tablespoons lemon juice
- Three cloves garlic, minced
- One teaspoon dried oregano
- One teaspoon dried basil
- 1/2 teaspoon dried thyme
- 1/2 teaspoon salt
- 1/4 teaspoon black pepper
- One red bell pepper, cut into chunks
- One yellow bell pepper, cut into chunks
- One red onion, cut into chunks
- Eight cherry tomatoes
- Wooden or metal skewers

Directions:

1. In a bowl, whisk together olive oil, lemon juice, minced garlic, dried oregano, dried basil, dried thyme, salt, and black pepper.
2. Add the chicken cubes to the bowl and toss them until they are well coated with the marinade. Let it marinate for at least 10 minutes, or you can refrigerate it for up to 4 hours for more flavour.
3. Preheat your grill to medium-high heat.
4. Thread the marinated chicken cubes onto skewers, alternating with the bell pepper chunks, onion chunks, and cherry tomatoes.

5. Place the skewers on the preheated grill and cook for about 6-8 minutes per side, or until the chicken is cooked through and the vegetables are slightly charred.
6. Remove the skewers from the grill and let them rest for a few minutes before serving.
7. Serve the grilled Mediterranean chicken skewers with your favourite side dishes or as part of a Mediterranean-inspired meal.

Nutrition Facts (per serving): Calories: 275 Total Fat: 12g Saturated Fat: 2g Cholesterol: 95mg Sodium: 360mg Carbohydrates: 7g Fiber: 2g Sugar: 3g Protein: 35g

Note: Nutrition facts are approximate and may vary depending on the specific ingredients and quantities used.

GRILLED CAESAR BURGER

Prep Time: 15 minutes Cooking Time: 10 minutes Serving: 4 burgers

Ingredients:
- 1 pound ground beef
- 1/4 cup grated Parmesan cheese
- 1/4 cup bread crumbs
- Two cloves garlic, minced
- One teaspoon Worcestershire sauce
- 1/2 teaspoon salt
- 1/4 teaspoon black pepper
- Four burger buns
- Four leaves romaine lettuce

- Four slices of bacon, cooked
- Caesar dressing
- Shredded Parmesan cheese for topping

Directions:

1. Preheat your grill to medium-high heat.
2. In a large mixing bowl, combine the ground beef, grated Parmesan cheese, bread crumbs, minced garlic, Worcestershire sauce, salt, and black pepper. Mix well until all the ingredients are evenly incorporated.
3. Divide the beef mixture into four equal portions and shape them into burger patties.
4. Place the burger patties on the preheated grill and cook for about 4-5 minutes per side or until they reach your desired level of doneness.
5. While the burgers are cooking, lightly toast the burger buns on the grill.
6. Once the burgers are cooked, remove them from the grill and let them rest for a couple of minutes.
7. To assemble the burgers, spread Caesar dressing on the bottom half of each burger bun. Place a grilled burger patty on top of the dressing.
8. Top each patty with a leaf of romaine lettuce, a slice of cooked bacon, and a sprinkle of shredded Parmesan cheese.
9. Finally, cover the burgers with the top half of the burger buns.
10. Serve the grilled Caesar burgers with your favourite side dishes, and enjoy!

Nutrition Facts (per serving):

- Calories: 450
- Total Fat: 23g
- Saturated Fat: 9g
- Cholesterol: 80mg
- Sodium: 920mg
- Carbohydrates: 29g
- Fibre: 2g
- Sugar: 3g
- Protein: 32g

Please note that these nutrition facts are approximate and may vary depending on the specific ingredients and brands used.

GRILLED HONEY LIME SALMON

Prep Time: 10 minutes Cooking Time: 12 minutes Serving: 4 servings

Ingredients:
- Four salmon fillets (about 6 ounces each)
- Three tablespoons honey
- Two tablespoons fresh lime juice
- Two tablespoons soy sauce
- Two cloves garlic, minced
- One teaspoon grated lime zest
- Salt and pepper to taste
- Lime wedges for garnish
- Fresh cilantro, chopped, for garnish

Directions:

1. Preheat your grill to medium-high heat.
2. In a small bowl, whisk together the honey, lime juice, soy sauce, minced garlic, lime zest, salt, and pepper until well combined.
3. Place the salmon fillets in a shallow dish or a resealable plastic bag. Pour the honey lime marinade over the salmon, ensuring each fillet is coated evenly. Allow the salmon to marinate for about 10 minutes.
4. Grease the grill grates with a bit of oil to prevent sticking. Place the salmon fillets on the grill, skin side down, and close the lid. Cook for about 6 minutes.
5. Carefully flip the salmon fillets using a spatula and continue grilling for another 5 to 6 minutes, or until the salmon is cooked through and flakes easily with a fork.
6. Remove the salmon from the grill and transfer it to a serving platter. Garnish with fresh cilantro and serve with lime wedges on the side.
7. Enjoy your delicious grilled honey lime salmon!

Nutrition Facts (per serving):
- Calories: 300
- Total Fat: 14g
- Saturated Fat: 2g
- Cholesterol: 80mg
- Sodium: 550mg
- Carbohydrates: 14g
- Fibre: 0.5g
- Sugar: 12g
- Protein: 30g

- Vitamin D: 10%
- Calcium: 2%
- Iron: 6%
- Potassium: 10%

BBQ BACON-WRAPPED SHRIMP

Prep Time: 15 minutes Cooking Time: 10 minutes Servings: 4

Ingredients:
- 24 large shrimp, peeled and deveined
- 12 slices of bacon
- 1/2 cup BBQ sauce
- One tablespoon olive oil
- Salt and pepper, to taste
- Wooden skewers, soaked in water for 30 minutes

Directions:
1. Preheat your grill to medium-high heat.
2. Season the shrimp with salt and pepper, then drizzle them with olive oil. Toss gently to coat the shrimp evenly.
3. Take each shrimp and wrap it with a slice of bacon. Secure the bacon with a wooden skewer, piercing through the shrimp. Repeat this process for all the shrimp.
4. Brush the bacon-wrapped shrimp generously with BBQ sauce, covering each piece.
5. Place the shrimp skewers on the preheated grill. Cook for about 4-5 minutes on each side or until the bacon is crispy and the shrimp is cooked through. Brush more BBQ sauce on the shrimp while grilling if desired.

6. Once cooked, remove the shrimp skewers from the grill and transfer them to a serving platter.
7. Serve the BBQ bacon-wrapped shrimp as an appetizer or as part of a main course. They go well with a side of coleslaw or grilled vegetables.

Nutrition Facts (per serving):
- Calories: 290
- Fat: 16g
- Saturated Fat: 4g
- Cholesterol: 230mg
- Sodium: 930mg
- Carbohydrates: 11g
- Sugar: 9g
- Protein: 25g

Note: The nutrition facts are approximate and may vary depending on the ingredients used.

Grilled Vegetable Pasta Salad

Prep Time: 20 minutes Cooking Time: 15 minutes Serving: 4

Ingredients:
- 8 ounces of pasta (penne, fusilli, or your choice)
- Two zucchinis, sliced lengthwise
- 1 red bell pepper, seeded and quartered
- One yellow bell pepper, seeded and quartered
- One red onion, sliced into thick rings
- 1 cup cherry tomatoes
- 1/4 cup extra-virgin olive oil

- Two cloves of garlic, minced
- Juice of 1 lemon
- 1/4 cup fresh basil leaves, chopped
- Salt and pepper to taste
- Grated Parmesan cheese (optional)

Directions:

1. Cook the pasta according to the package instructions until al dente. Drain and set aside.
2. Preheat your grill to medium-high heat.
3. In a large bowl, toss the sliced zucchini, red and yellow bell peppers, red onion rings, cherry tomatoes with olive oil, minced garlic, salt, and pepper.
4. Place the vegetables on the preheated grill and cook for about 3-4 minutes per side or until they are charred and tender. Remove from the grill and let them cool slightly.
5. Chop the grilled vegetables into bite-sized pieces and transfer them to a large mixing bowl.
6. Add the cooked pasta to the bowl with the grilled vegetables.
7. Drizzle the lemon juice over the pasta and vegetables, then add the chopped basil leaves. Toss gently to combine.
8. Season with additional salt and pepper if needed.
9. Serve the grilled vegetable pasta salad warm or at room temperature. If desired, sprinkle some grated Parmesan cheese on top.

Nutrition Facts (per serving): Calories: 320 Total Fat: 12g Saturated Fat: 2g Cholesterol: 0mg Sodium: 150mg Total Carbohydrate: 48g Dietary Fiber: 6g Sugar: 8g Protein: 8g

Note: Nutritional values are approximate and may vary depending on the ingredients used.

LEMON HERB GRILLED PORK CHOPS

Prep Time: 10 minutes Cooking Time: 15 minutes Serving: 4 servings

Ingredients:

- Four boneless pork chops
- Two lemons
- Three cloves of garlic, minced
- Two tablespoons fresh herbs (such as rosemary, thyme, or oregano), chopped
- Two tablespoons olive oil
- Salt and pepper to taste

Directions:

1. Preheat your grill to medium-high heat.
2. In a small bowl, squeeze the juice from one lemon and add the minced garlic, chopped herbs, olive oil, salt, and pepper. Mix well to combine.
3. Place the pork chops in a shallow dish and pour the marinade over them. Make sure the chops are evenly coated. Let them marinate for about 10 minutes while the grill is preheating.
4. Once the grill is hot, remove the pork chops from the marinade, allowing any excess to drip off. Reserve the marinade for basting.
5. Place the pork chops on the grill and cook for about 6-8 minutes per side or until they reach an internal temperature

of 145°F (63°C). While grilling, baste the chops occasionally with the reserved marinade.
6. While the pork chops are grilling, slice the remaining lemon into wedges for serving.
7. Once the pork chops are cooked, remove them from the grill and let them rest for a few minutes.
8. Serve the lemon herb grilled pork chops with the lemon wedges on the side. They pair well with steamed vegetables, roasted potatoes, or a fresh salad.

Nutrition Facts (per serving):
- Calories: 250
- Fat: 14g
- Saturated Fat: 3.5g
- Cholesterol: 75mg
- Sodium: 70mg
- Carbohydrates: 4g
- Fibre: 1g
- Sugar: 1g
- Protein: 27g

Note: Nutrition facts may vary depending on the specific ingredients and brands used.

GRILLED VEGGIE FAJITAS

Prep Time: 20 minutes Cooking Time: 15 minutes Serving: 4 servings

Ingredients:
- Two bell peppers (any colour), sliced

- One large red onion, sliced
- Two zucchinis, sliced
- Two yellow squash, sliced
- 1 cup sliced mushrooms
- Three tablespoons olive oil
- Two cloves garlic, minced
- One teaspoon ground cumin
- 1 teaspoon chilli powder
- 1/2 teaspoon paprika
- 1/2 teaspoon salt
- 1/4 teaspoon black pepper
- Eight small flour tortillas
- Salsa, guacamole, and sour cream for serving (optional)

Directions:

1. Preheat your grill to medium-high heat.
2. In a large bowl, combine the sliced bell peppers, red onion, zucchini, yellow squash, and mushrooms.
3. In a small bowl, whisk together the olive oil, minced garlic, cumin, chilli powder, paprika, salt, and black pepper. Pour the marinade over the vegetables and toss to coat them evenly.
4. Place the marinated vegetables on a grill pan or directly on the grill grates, ensuring they are spread out in a single layer.
5. Grill the vegetables for about 10-15 minutes, flipping them occasionally, until they are tender and slightly charred.

6. While the vegetables are grilling, warm the flour tortillas on the grill or in a dry skillet for a few seconds on each side until they are pliable.
7. Remove the grilled vegetables from the heat and transfer them to a serving dish.
8. Serve the grilled vegetables with warm tortillas and your choice of salsa, guacamole, and sour cream.
9. To assemble a fajita, place a spoonful of grilled vegetables in the centre of a tortilla, fold the sides over the filling, and roll it up tightly.
10. Enjoy your delicious grilled veggie fajitas!

Nutrition Facts (per serving):
- Calories: 250
- Fat: 10g
- Carbohydrates: 35g
- Fibre: 5g
- Protein: 6g
- Vitamin C: 80% of the Daily Value
- Vitamin A: 15% of the Daily Value
- Iron: 10% of the Daily Value
- Calcium: 6% of the Daily Value

Please note that the nutrition facts may vary depending on the specific brands and quantities of ingredients used.

BBQ CHICKEN FLATBREAD PIZZA

Prep Time: 20 minutes Cooking Time: 15 minutes Serving: 4 servings

Ingredients:
- Two pre-made flatbreads or pizza crusts
- 1 cup BBQ sauce
- 2 cups cooked chicken, shredded or diced
- 1 cup red onion, thinly sliced
- 1 cup mozzarella cheese, shredded
- 1/4 cup fresh cilantro, chopped (optional)

Directions:
1. Preheat your oven to 425°F (220°C).
2. Place the flatbreads or pizza crusts on a baking sheet or pizza stone.
3. Spread BBQ sauce evenly over each flatbread or crust, leaving a small border around the edges.
4. Sprinkle the cooked chicken evenly over the BBQ sauce.
5. Scatter the sliced red onion over the chicken.
6. Sprinkle the shredded mozzarella cheese over the top.
7. Place the baking sheet or pizza stone in the preheated oven and bake for about 12-15 minutes, or until the cheese is melted and bubbly and the edges of the flatbread are golden brown.
8. Remove the pizzas from the oven and let them cool for a few minutes.
9. Garnish with chopped cilantro, if desired.
10. Cut each flatbread or pizza into slices and serve hot.

Nutrition Facts (per serving):
- Calories: 380
- Fat: 10g

- Saturated Fat: 4g
- Cholesterol: 70mg
- Sodium: 890mg
- Carbohydrates: 46g
- Fibre: 3g
- Sugar: 19g
- Protein: 27g

Note: Nutrition facts may vary depending on the specific brands of ingredients used and any modifications made to the recipe.

GRILLED CILANTRO LIME SHRIMP TACOS

Prep Time: 20 minutes Cooking Time: 10 minutes Serving: 4

Ingredients:
- 1 pound large shrimp, peeled and deveined
- Two tablespoons of olive oil
- Juice of 2 limes
- Zest of 1 lime
- Three cloves garlic, minced
- 1/4 cup fresh cilantro, chopped
- One teaspoon chilli powder
- 1/2 teaspoon ground cumin
- Salt and pepper, to taste
- Eight small flour tortillas
- 1 cup shredded lettuce
- 1/2 cup diced tomatoes
- 1/2 cup diced red onion
- 1/4 cup sour cream
- Lime wedges for serving

Directions:
1. Preheat your grill to medium-high heat.
2. In a large bowl, combine the olive oil, lime juice, zest, minced garlic, chopped cilantro, chilli powder, ground cumin, salt, and pepper. Mix well to make a marinade.
3. Add the shrimp to the marinade and toss until well-coated. Allow the shrimp to marinate for 10 minutes.

4. While the shrimp is marinating, prepare the tortillas. Wrap them in aluminium foil and place them on the grill to warm them up for a few minutes. Alternatively, you can warm them in a dry skillet over medium heat on the stovetop.
5. Thread the marinated shrimp onto skewers, or use a grill basket to cook them. Grill the shrimp for about 2-3 minutes per side until they are opaque and cooked through.
6. Remove the shrimp from the grill and let them cool slightly. Remove the shrimp from the skewers if using.
7. To assemble the tacos, place a few shrimp on each warmed tortilla. Top with shredded lettuce, diced tomatoes, and diced red onion. Drizzle with sour cream and sprinkle with additional chopped cilantro if desired.
8. Serve the Grilled Cilantro Lime Shrimp Tacos with lime wedges on the side to squeeze extra lime juice over the tacos.

Nutrition Facts: (Note: Nutritional information may vary depending on the specific ingredients and brands used)

Serving Size: 1 taco Calories: Approximately 250 Total Fat: 10g Saturated Fat: 2g Cholesterol: 160mg Sodium: 350mg Carbohydrates: 22g Fiber: 2g Sugar: 2g Protein: 18g

Enjoy your delicious Grilled Cilantro Lime Shrimp Tacos!

BBQ Chicken Flatbread with Caramelized Onions

Prep Time: 15 minutes Cooking Time: 25 minutes Serving: 4 servings

Ingredients:
- Four flatbreads
- 2 cups cooked chicken, shredded

- 1 cup BBQ sauce
- Two large onions, thinly sliced
- Two tablespoons of olive oil
- Salt and pepper to taste
- 2 cups shredded mozzarella cheese
- Fresh cilantro leaves for garnish

Directions:

1. Preheat the oven to 400°F (200°C).
2. Heat the olive oil in a large skillet over medium heat. Add the sliced onions and cook until caramelized, stirring occasionally, for about 10-15 minutes. Season with salt and pepper to taste.
3. Heat the BBQ sauce over low heat in a small saucepan until warm.
4. Place the flatbreads on a baking sheet. Spread a layer of warm BBQ sauce over each flatbread.
5. Evenly distribute the shredded chicken over the flatbreads, followed by the caramelized onions.
6. Sprinkle the shredded mozzarella cheese over the top of each flatbread.
7. Bake in the preheated oven for about 10 minutes or until the cheese is melted and bubbly.
8. Remove from the oven and let the flatbreads cool slightly. Garnish with fresh cilantro leaves.
9. Slice the flatbreads into desired portions and serve hot.

Nutrition Facts (per serving):

- Calories: 420
- Fat: 18g

- Saturated Fat: 7g
- Cholesterol: 73mg
- Sodium: 924mg
- Carbohydrates: 39g
- Fibre: 3g
- Sugar: 15g
- Protein: 25g

Note: Nutrition facts are approximate and may vary depending on the ingredients used.

GRILLED LEMON HERB PORK TENDERLOIN

Prep Time: 15 minutes Cooking Time: 20 minutes Serving: 4 servings

Ingredients:
- Two pork tenderloins (about 1 pound each)
- Two lemons, juiced and zested
- Three tablespoons olive oil
- Four cloves garlic, minced
- Two teaspoons dried thyme
- Two teaspoons dried rosemary
- Salt and pepper, to taste

Directions:
1. In a small bowl, whisk together the lemon juice, lemon zest, olive oil, minced garlic, dried thyme, rosemary, salt, and pepper.
2. Place the pork tenderloins in a shallow dish or a resealable plastic bag. Pour the marinade over the pork, making sure it

is well coated. Marinate in the refrigerator for at least 1 hour or overnight for better flavour.

3. Preheat your grill to medium-high heat.
4. Remove the pork tenderloins from the marinade and discard the excess marinade.
5. Place the pork tenderloins on the preheated grill and cook for about 10 minutes on each side or until the internal temperature reaches 145°F (63°C). Cooking time may vary depending on the thickness of the tenderloins.
6. Once cooked, transfer the pork tenderloins to a cutting board and let them rest for 5 minutes before slicing.
7. Slice the grilled pork tenderloins into ½-inch thick slices and serve hot.

Nutrition Facts (per serving):
- Calories: 280
- Total Fat: 13g
- Saturated Fat: 3g
- Cholesterol: 120mg
- Sodium: 170mg
- Carbohydrates: 4g
- Fibre: 1g
- Sugar: 0g
- Protein: 35g

Note: Nutrition facts are approximate and may vary depending on the ingredients used.

BACON-WRAPPED BBQ MEATBALLS

Prep Time: 15 minutes Cooking Time: 25 minutes Serving: 4-6 servings

Ingredients:

- 1 pound ground beef
- 1/2 cup bread crumbs
- 1/4 cup milk
- 1/4 cup grated Parmesan cheese
- 1/4 cup finely chopped onion
- One clove garlic, minced
- One teaspoon dried oregano
- 1/2 teaspoon salt
- 1/4 teaspoon black pepper
- 1/2 cup BBQ sauce
- 12 slices bacon

Directions:

1. Preheat the oven to 375°F (190°C). Line a baking sheet with aluminium foil and set aside.
2. In a large mixing bowl, combine ground beef, bread crumbs, milk, Parmesan cheese, onion, garlic, oregano, salt, and black pepper. Mix well until all the ingredients are evenly incorporated.
3. Shape the meat mixture into small meatballs, about 1 inch in diameter. You should get approximately 24 meatballs.
4. Wrap each meatball with a slice of bacon and secure it with a toothpick. Place the bacon-wrapped meatballs on the prepared baking sheet.
5. Bake in the preheated oven for 20 minutes or until the bacon is crispy and the meatballs are cooked.

6. Remove the toothpicks from the meatballs and transfer them to a clean baking dish. Pour BBQ sauce over the meatballs, ensuring each one is coated with sauce.
7. Return the meatballs to the oven and bake for 5 minutes, allowing the sauce to heat through.
8. Serve the bacon-wrapped BBQ meatballs as an appetizer or as a main course with your favourite side dishes.

Nutrition Facts (per serving):

- Calories: 285
- Total Fat: 16g
- Saturated Fat: 6g
- Cholesterol: 57mg
- Sodium: 876mg
- Total Carbohydrate: 17g
- Dietary Fiber: 1g
- Sugars: 8g
- Protein: 18g

Note: The nutrition facts are approximate and may vary depending on the specific ingredients and quantities used.

GRILLED TERIYAKI VEGETABLE FRIED RICE

Prep Time: 15 minutes Cooking Time: 20 minutes Serving: 4 servings

Ingredients:

- 2 cups cooked rice (preferably day-old)
- Two tablespoons vegetable oil
- One small onion, diced

- Two cloves garlic, minced
- 1 cup mixed vegetables (such as carrots, peas, corn)
- 1 cup broccoli florets
- 1 cup sliced bell peppers (any colour)
- 1 cup grilled teriyaki tofu, diced
- Two tablespoons soy sauce
- Two tablespoons teriyaki sauce
- One tablespoon sesame oil
- Two green onions, sliced
- Sesame seeds (optional, for garnish)

Directions:

1. Heat vegetable oil in a large skillet or wok over medium heat. Add diced onions and minced garlic, and sauté until onions become translucent.
2. Add mixed vegetables, broccoli florets, and bell peppers to the skillet. Stir-fry for about 5 minutes until the vegetables are tender-crisp.
3. Push the vegetables to one side of the skillet and add the diced teriyaki tofu to the space. Cook for 2-3 minutes to heat through.
4. Add cooked rice to the skillet and mix well with the vegetables and tofu.
5. Whisk together soy sauce, teriyaki sauce, and sesame oil in a small bowl. Pour the sauce mixture over the rice and vegetables, and stir-fry for another 2-3 minutes until everything is well coated and heated through.
6. Remove from heat and garnish with sliced green onions and sesame seeds, if desired.

7. Serve the Grilled Teriyaki Vegetable Fried Rice hot, and enjoy!

Nutrition Facts (per serving):

- Calories: 320
- Fat: 10g
- Carbohydrates: 48g
- Protein: 10g
- Fibre: 4g
- Sugar: 6g
- Sodium: 600mg

Note: Nutrition facts may vary depending on the specific ingredients and brands used.

GRILLED MEDITERRANEAN STUFFED PEPPERS

Prep Time: 20 minutes Cooking Time: 30 minutes Serving: 4 servings

Ingredients:

- Four large bell peppers (any colour)
- 1 cup cooked quinoa
- 1 cup chopped cherry tomatoes
- 1/2 cup crumbled feta cheese
- 1/4 cup chopped Kalamata olives
- 1/4 cup chopped fresh parsley
- Two tablespoons chopped fresh basil
- Two tablespoons olive oil
- Two cloves garlic, minced

- One teaspoon dried oregano
- Salt and pepper to taste

Directions:

1. Preheat the grill to medium-high heat.
2. Cut the tops off the bell peppers and remove the seeds and membranes. Rinse them under cold water and set them aside.
3. In a mixing bowl, combine the cooked quinoa, cherry tomatoes, feta cheese, Kalamata olives, parsley, basil, olive oil, garlic, dried oregano, salt, and pepper. Mix well until all the ingredients are evenly distributed.
4. Stuff each bell pepper with the quinoa mixture, pressing it down gently. Make sure to fill the peppers.
5. Place the stuffed peppers on the preheated grill and close the lid. Cook for about 15-20 minutes or until the peppers are tender and slightly charred. You can rotate the peppers occasionally for even cooking.
6. Once cooked, remove the stuffed peppers from the grill and let them cool for a few minutes.
7. Serve the grilled Mediterranean stuffed peppers warm as a main dish or a side dish. You can garnish them with additional chopped fresh herbs if desired.

Nutrition Facts (per serving):

- Calories: 250
- Fat: 12g
- Saturated Fat: 4g
- Cholesterol: 17mg
- Sodium: 410mg

- Carbohydrates: 28g
- Fibre: 5g
- Sugar: 6g
- Protein: 9g

Note: Nutrition facts may vary depending on the specific ingredients and brands used.

BBQ BACON-WRAPPED STUFFED CHICKEN BREASTS

Prep Time: 15 minutes Cooking Time: 30 minutes Serving: 4 servings

Ingredients:

- Four boneless, skinless chicken breasts
- Eight slices of bacon
- 1 cup shredded mozzarella cheese
- 1 cup baby spinach leaves
- 1/2 cup barbecue sauce
- One tablespoon olive oil
- Salt and pepper to taste

Directions:

1. Preheat the oven to 375°F (190°C). Line a baking sheet with foil and set aside.
2. Using a sharp knife, make a horizontal slit in the thickest part of each chicken breast to create a pocket for the stuffing. Be careful not to cut all the way through.
3. Season the inside of each chicken breast with salt and pepper.

4. Stuff each chicken breast with an equal amount of shredded mozzarella cheese and baby spinach leaves. Press the edges of the chicken breasts together to seal the stuffing inside.
5. Wrap each stuffed chicken breast with two slices of bacon, ensuring that the bacon covers the entire surface of the chicken.
6. In a large skillet, heat the olive oil over medium-high heat. Sear the bacon-wrapped chicken breasts for 2-3 minutes on each side until the bacon is slightly crispy.
7. Transfer the chicken breasts to the prepared baking sheet and brush each breast with barbecue sauce.
8. Bake in the preheated oven for 20-25 minutes or until the chicken is cooked and the bacon is crispy.
9. Remove from the oven and let the chicken breasts rest for a few minutes before serving.
10. Serve the BBQ bacon-wrapped stuffed chicken breasts with additional barbecue sauce on the side if desired.

Nutrition Facts (per serving):

- Calories: 425
- Fat: 22g
- Saturated Fat: 8g
- Cholesterol: 128mg
- Sodium: 855mg
- Carbohydrates: 10g
- Fibre: 1g
- Sugar: 7g
- Protein: 46g

Note: The nutrition facts are approximate and may vary depending on the ingredients used.

GRILLED HONEY SRIRACHA WINGS

Prep Time: 10 minutes Cooking Time: 25 minutes Serving: 4 servings

Ingredients:

- 2 pounds of chicken wings
- 1/4 cup honey
- Two tablespoons sriracha sauce
- Two tablespoons soy sauce
- Two tablespoons lime juice
- Two cloves garlic, minced
- One teaspoon grated ginger
- Salt and pepper to taste
- Chopped green onions for garnish

Directions:

1. Preheat your grill to medium-high heat.
2. In a bowl, combine honey, sriracha sauce, soy sauce, lime juice, minced garlic, grated ginger, salt, and pepper. Mix well to make the marinade.
3. Place the chicken wings in a large resealable plastic bag or a bowl. Pour the marinade over the wings, ensuring they are well coated. Marinate for at least 30 minutes or overnight for better flavour.
4. Remove the wings from the marinade, allowing any excess marinade to drip off.

5. Grill the wings on the preheated grill for about 12-15 minutes per side or until they are cooked through and have a nice charred appearance.
6. While grilling, baste the wings occasionally with the remaining marinade to enhance the flavour.
7. Once the wings are cooked, remove them from the grill and transfer them to a serving platter. Sprinkle chopped green onions over the wings for garnish.
8. Serve the Grilled Honey Sriracha Wings hot as an appetizer or as part of a main course.

Nutrition Facts (per serving):

- Calories: 320
- Fat: 18g
- Carbohydrates: 16g
- Protein: 24g
- Fibre: 0.5g
- Sugar: 14g
- Sodium: 780mg
- Cholesterol: 90mg

Note: The nutrition facts provided are approximate values and may vary depending on the specific ingredients used.

TERIYAKI GLAZED GRILLED PINEAPPLE CHICKEN SKEWERS

Prep Time: 20 minutes Cooking Time: 15 minutes Serving: 4 servings

Ingredients:

- 1 pound boneless, skinless chicken breasts cut into 1-inch cubes
- 1 cup teriyaki sauce
- 1/4 cup pineapple juice
- Two tablespoons honey
- One tablespoon soy sauce
- Two cloves garlic, minced
- One teaspoon grated fresh ginger
- 1/2 teaspoon red pepper flakes (optional)
- One fresh pineapple, peeled, cored, and cut into chunks
- One red bell pepper, cut into chunks
- One green bell pepper, cut into chunks
- One red onion, cut into chunks
- Wooden skewers, soaked in water for 30 minutes

Directions:

1. In a bowl, whisk together teriyaki sauce, pineapple juice, honey, soy sauce, minced garlic, grated ginger, and red pepper flakes (if using). Reserve half of the marinade for basting.
2. Place the chicken cubes in a large resealable plastic bag and pour the remaining marinade over them. Seal the bag and marinate in the refrigerator for at least 1 hour, preferably overnight.
3. Preheat your grill to medium-high heat.
4. Thread the marinated chicken, pineapple chunks, bell peppers, and onion onto the soaked wooden skewers, alternating the ingredients.

5. Place the skewers on the preheated grill and cook for about 6-8 minutes per side, or until the chicken is cooked and the vegetables are slightly charred, basting occasionally with the reserved marinade.
6. Remove the skewers from the grill and let them rest for a few minutes before serving.
7. Serve the Teriyaki Glazed Grilled Pineapple Chicken Skewers hot with steamed rice or a side salad.

Nutrition Facts (per serving):
- Calories: 320
- Total Fat: 4g
- Saturated Fat: 1g
- Cholesterol: 75mg
- Sodium: 1800mg
- Carbohydrates: 40g
- Fibre: 3g
- Sugar: 32g
- Protein: 32g

Note: The nutrition facts provided are estimates and may vary based on the specific ingredients used.

GRILLED GREEK LAMB BURGERS

Prep Time: 15 minutes Cooking Time: 12 minutes Serving: 4 burgers

Ingredients:
- 1 pound ground lamb
- 1/2 cup crumbled feta cheese

- 1/4 cup finely chopped red onion
- Two cloves garlic, minced
- 1/4 cup chopped fresh parsley
- One teaspoon dried oregano
- 1/2 teaspoon ground cumin
- 1/2 teaspoon salt
- 1/4 teaspoon black pepper
- Four burger buns
- Tzatziki sauce (optional for serving)
- Sliced tomatoes, lettuce, and red onion (optional, for serving)

Directions:

1. Preheat the grill to medium-high heat.
2. In a large bowl, combine the ground lamb, feta cheese, red onion, garlic, parsley, oregano, cumin, salt, and black pepper. Mix well to combine all the ingredients.
3. Divide the mixture into four equal portions and shape each portion into a patty about 3/4-inch thick.
4. Place the lamb patties on the preheated grill. Cook for about 6 minutes per side or until the internal temperature reaches 160°F (71°C) for medium doneness.
5. While the patties are cooking, lightly toast the burger buns on the grill.
6. Remove the lamb patties from the grill and let them rest for a few minutes.
7. Assemble the burgers by placing each patty on a toasted bun. If desired, top with a spoonful of tzatziki sauce, sliced tomatoes, lettuce, and red onion.

8. Serve the Grilled Greek Lamb Burgers immediately, and enjoy!

Nutrition Facts (per serving):
- Calories: 420
- Total Fat: 24g
- Saturated Fat: 10g
- Cholesterol: 95mg
- Sodium: 670mg
- Carbohydrates: 24g
- Fibre: 2g
- Sugars: 4g
- Protein: 26g

Note: The nutrition facts may vary depending on the specific ingredients and brands used.

BBQ PULLED CHICKEN SLIDERS WITH COLESLAW

Prep Time: 15 minutes Cooking Time: 4 hours Serving: 6-8 servings

Ingredients:
- 2 pounds boneless, skinless chicken breasts
- 1 cup barbecue sauce
- 1/4 cup apple cider vinegar
- 1/4 cup brown sugar
- 1/4 cup chicken broth
- One teaspoon smoked paprika
- 1/2 teaspoon garlic powder

- 1/2 teaspoon onion powder
- Salt and pepper to taste
- 12-16 slider buns

For the Coleslaw:
- 4 cups shredded cabbage
- 1/2 cup mayonnaise
- Two tablespoons apple cider vinegar
- One tablespoon Dijon mustard
- One tablespoon honey
- Salt and pepper to taste

Directions:
1. In a slow cooker, combine barbecue sauce, apple cider vinegar, brown sugar, chicken broth, smoked paprika, garlic powder, onion powder, salt, and pepper. Stir well to combine.
2. Add the chicken breasts to the slow cooker and coat them evenly with the sauce mixture.
3. Cover the slow cooker and cook on low heat for 4 hours or until the chicken is tender and easily shreddable.
4. Once the chicken is cooked, remove it from the slow cooker and shred it using two forks.
5. Return the shredded chicken to the slow cooker and mix it with the sauce.
6. In a separate bowl, prepare the coleslaw by combining shredded cabbage, mayonnaise, apple cider vinegar, Dijon mustard, honey, salt, and pepper. Toss well to coat the cabbage evenly.

7. To assemble the sliders, place a generous amount of BBQ-pulled chicken on the bottom half of each slider bun.
8. Top the chicken with a spoonful of coleslaw.
9. Place the top half of the bun over the coleslaw to complete the sliders.
10. Serve the BBQ-pulled chicken sliders with coleslaw immediately.

Nutrition Facts (per serving):
- Calories: 350
- Fat: 12g
- Saturated Fat: 2g
- Cholesterol: 75mg
- Sodium: 600mg
- Carbohydrates: 37g
- Fibre: 2g
- Sugar: 18g
- Protein: 25g

Note: The nutrition facts are approximate and may vary depending on the specific ingredients and brands used.

GRILLED TERIYAKI TOFU STIR-FRY

Prep Time: 15 minutes Cooking Time: 20 minutes Serving: 4 servings

Ingredients:
- One block of firm tofu, drained and pressed
- 1/4 cup soy sauce
- 1/4 cup teriyaki sauce

- Two tablespoons rice vinegar
- Two tablespoons brown sugar
- Two cloves garlic, minced
- One tablespoon grated ginger
- Two tablespoons vegetable oil
- One red bell pepper, sliced
- One yellow bell pepper, sliced
- One medium zucchini, sliced
- 1 cup broccoli florets
- 1 cup snap peas
- 1 cup sliced mushrooms
- Cooked rice or noodles for serving
- Sesame seeds, for garnish
- Green onions, sliced, for garnish

Directions:

1. In a bowl, combine the soy sauce, teriyaki sauce, rice vinegar, brown sugar, minced garlic, and grated ginger. Whisk until well combined.
2. Cut the pressed tofu into bite-sized cubes and place them in a shallow dish. Pour half of the teriyaki marinade over the tofu and gently toss to coat. Set aside for 10 minutes to marinate.
3. Heat one tablespoon of vegetable oil in a large skillet or wok over medium-high heat. Add the marinated tofu to the skillet and cook for 5-7 minutes, stirring occasionally, until the tofu is golden brown and crispy. Remove the tofu from the skillet and set aside.

4. In the same skillet, add another tablespoon of vegetable oil. Add the sliced bell peppers, zucchini, broccoli florets, snap peas, and sliced mushrooms. Stir-fry the vegetables for 5-6 minutes until they are crisp-tender.
5. Pour the remaining teriyaki marinade over the vegetables and stir to coat. Cook for an additional 2 minutes, allowing the sauce to thicken slightly.
6. Add the cooked tofu back to the skillet and toss to combine with the vegetables and sauce. Cook for an additional 2 minutes to heat through.
7. Serve the grilled teriyaki tofu stir-fry over cooked rice or noodles. Garnish with sesame seeds and sliced green onions.

Nutrition Facts (per serving):
- Calories: 250
- Total Fat: 10g
- Saturated Fat: 1.5g
- Cholesterol: 0mg
- Sodium: 1000mg
- Total Carbohydrate: 30g
- Dietary Fiber: 5g
- Sugars: 15g
- Protein: 12g

Note: The nutrition facts may vary depending on the specific brands of ingredients used and any modifications made to the recipe.

CONCLUSION

In conclusion, the "Blackstone Outdoor Gas Griddle Cookbook: 1000 Days Mouthwatering, Delicious Recipes and Expert Tips for Mastering Your Grill" is a must-have for outdoor cooking enthusiasts. With its extensive recipe collection, expert tips, and comprehensive guide, this cookbook provides everything you need to take your griddle cooking skills to the next level.

From breakfast to dinner and everything in between, the cookbook offers a diverse range of recipes that will tantalize your taste buds and impress your guests. Whether you're grilling succulent meats, creating flavorful stir-fries, or indulging in delightful desserts, the cookbook has a recipe for every occasion.

The expert tips and techniques shared throughout the book will empower you to become a master of your Blackstone outdoor gas grill. You'll learn how to achieve optimal heat control, create perfect sear marks, and maintain your grill for long-lasting performance.

The cookbook goes beyond just recipes and tips by providing a comprehensive guide that covers all aspects of outdoor griddle cooking. You'll learn about griddle setup, essential tools and accessories, and proper maintenance and cleaning techniques. This knowledge will help you make the most of your skillet and ensure its longevity.

The captivating food photography within the cookbook will inspire and motivate you to try new flavours and presentations. The vibrant visuals bring the recipes to life, making your culinary journey even more enjoyable.

Whether you're a seasoned griller or a beginner, the "Blackstone Outdoor Gas Griddle Cookbook" is an invaluable resource that will ignite your passion for outdoor cooking and help you create unforgettable meals. With its mouthwatering recipes, expert tips, and stunning visuals, this cookbook is a true companion for mastering your Blackstone gas griddle. Get ready to embark on a culinary adventure that will leave your taste buds satisfied and your friends and family impressed.

Made in United States
Troutdale, OR
10/27/2023